UNIFIED ACTION HANDBOOK SERIES

This *Handbook for Military Support to Essential Services and Critical Infrastructure* is Book Two in a set of five handbooks developed to assist the joint force commander design, plan, and execute a whole-of-government approach. Included with the series is an overview J7/J9 Pamphlet, *Executive Summary of the Unified Action Handbook Series*, that describes the handbooks, suggests how they should be used, and identifies the significant interrelationships among them. The following is a short summary of each handbook:

Book One: *Military Participation in the Interagency Management System for Reconstruction and Stabilization*

The handbook outlines joint force roles and responsibilities in the Interagency Management System (IMS) and existing interagency coordination authorities and mechanisms. It aligns with the *USG Planning Framework for Reconstruction, Stabilization, and Conflict Transformation*. It will also align with the *IMS Guide* under development at the Department of States's Office of the Coordinator for Reconstruction and Stabilization.

Book Two: *Military Support to Essential Services and Critical Infrastructure*

This handbook defines services essential to sustain human life during stability operations (water, sanitation, transportation, medical, etc.), the infrastructure needed to deliver such services, and potential joint force responsibilities.

Book Three: *Military Support to Governance, Elections, and Media*

The last comprehensive guide to military governance was written in 1943. Combatant commanders have directed joint forces to rebuild media, support election preparations, and provide advisors to embryonic executive ministries and legislative committees in recent and current operations. This handbook provides pre-doctrinal guidance for joint force support to good governance, political competition, and support to media.

Book Four: *Military Support to Economic Stabilization*

This handbook outlines joint force support to economic development. It addresses conducting a comprehensive economic assessment, employment and business generation, trade, agriculture, financial sector development and regulation, and legal transformation.

Book Five: *Military Support to Rule of Law and Security Sector Reform*

This handbook defines the "Rule of Law;" explains the interrelationship between rule of law, governance, and security; and provides a template to analyze the rule of law foundation essential to successful stability operations.

NOTICE TO USERS

All approved and current Joint Warfighting Center (JWFC) Pamphlets, Handbooks, and White Papers are posted on the Joint Doctrine, Education, and Training Electronic Information System (JDEIS) Web page at https:// jdeis.js.mil/jdeis/jel/template.jsp?title=jwfcpam&filename =jwfc_pam.htm. If a JWFC product is not posted there; it is either in development or rescinded.

PREFACE

1. Scope

This *Handbook for Military Support to Essential Services and Critical Infrastructure* provides fundamental guidance, planning considerations, techniques, and procedures for the development of essential services and critical infrastructure (ES&CI) during Phase 0, "Shaping" operations or restoration of ES&CI in the wake of a natural disaster or combat during joint operation phases IV, "Stabilize," and V, "Enable Civil Authority."

2. Purpose

This handbook is not intended to stand alone as a planning guide, but instead to complement the planning that would be required to better integrate all elements of national capacity in response to an overseas contingency or in support of military engagement, security cooperation, and deterrence activities. **Its primary purpose is to provide guidance for joint force commanders and military planners during the post-conflict period, since the military likely will continue to contribute to ES&CI restoration throughout the post-conflict period**. It is designed to help lay the groundwork for a successful transition between military and civilian authorities in situations where the armed forces for whatever reason find themselves as the *de facto* governing authority responsible for providing essential governmental services for a civilian population. It is titled to emphasize that although infrastructure projects provide visible evidence of progress and represent a straightforward engineering problem, their larger purpose is to support delivery of some particular governmental or community-wide service.

3. Background and Content

a. In conventional war one objective is to destroy the infrastructure that the adversary uses to support its combat effort. In today's conflicts, a principal objective is to win the confidence of the population and convert the adversary to become a partner who contributes to stability. The preservation and development of the critical infrastructure to function effectively and serve the needs of the population is an important component in winning the confidence and support of the population. Thus, judgment on how to limit the destruction of infrastructure is important to support rapid post-conflict recovery.

b. Once large-scale combat concludes, recent experience (e.g., Operations ENDURING FREEDOM and IRAQI FREEDOM) has demonstrated that the same military units conducting the combat will likely remain to initiate post-conflict restoration of ES&CI. It is in the initial portion of the post-conflict period, with uncertain security conditions for civilians, that the military may bear significant responsibility for ES&CI restoration.

c. This handbook defines the services (water, sanitation, transportation, medical, etc.) needed to sustain civilian populations, the infrastructure needed to deliver such services, why delivery of such services is critical, and the appropriate roles military forces can play to enable service delivery. It describes the nature of the situations that will be faced and provides both general guidance on addressing recovery problems and contact references to obtain specialized assistance. It covers both steady-state Phase 0 and post-conflict Phases IV and V ES&CI-related operations. It stresses that civilians are generally the supported entity for ES&CI-related operations, and urges that where security conditions inhibit civilian deployment they be invited to embed with military units to the extent possible.

4. Development

a. JP 1-02, *Department of Defense Dictionary of Military and Associated Terms*, defines unified action as, "The synchronization, coordination, and/or integration of the activities of governmental and nongovernmental entities with military operations to achieve unity of effort." To this end, United States Joint Forces Command (USJFCOM) embarked on a multi-year "Unified Action" project to carry forward the principles of unified action through concept development and experimentation. This project focused on two lines of operations (LOOs) to achieve its objectives. The first line included limited objective experiments contributing to the implementation of the DOD work plan to support National Security Presidential Directive 44 (NSPD-44). The second LOO included spiral events to produce a series of handbooks and overview (see inside of the front cover). The products of both LOOs were developed and validated through a rigorous process of experimentation that was conducted with military and civilian partners across the United States Government.

b. This handbook was developed in close coordination with, and used significant input from, both civilian and military subject matter experts. The authors also regularly vetted the content with these experts to assure currency and accuracy of both theory and practice. As a result, it represent the current state of best practices in ES&CI development and restoration.

c. An important issue which arose during the drafting of this handbook is the widespread use of jargon and acronyms that may not translate particularly well between various agencies within the US Government. Insofar as possible, the authors have attempted to improve the readability of this handbook by using common terms in plain English. Additionally, "steady state" is utilized by the US Department of State to describe the full range of engagement with host nations in a non-crisis environment.[1] This handbook also includes a glossary of terms commonly used within the interagency community that may not be familiar to military planners.

d. The following key individuals provided crucial inputs in defining and scoping this handbook:

- Mr. Allen Eisendrath, United States Agency for International Development (USAID) (EGAT/I&E) spearheads a comprehensive annual infrastructure conference for USAID's worldwide staff.

- Ms. Peggy Meites from USAID's Global Health Branch provided perspectives on health sector considerations during an intervention.

- Mrs. Debra Boline, Naval Surface Warfare Center, Dahlgren, VA, provided extensive time, advice, and materials outlining the importance and level of detail required for effective infrastructure assessments. The Defense Critical Infrastructure Program reflects her comprehensive understanding of the infrastructure sector.

5. Application

This handbook is not approved joint doctrine, but is a non-authoritative supplement to current stability operations doctrine that can assist commanders and their staffs in planning, executing, and assessing ES&CI development and restoration activities. The information herein also can help the joint community develop stability operations doctrine, mature ES&CI concepts for possible transition into joint doctrine, and further the effectiveness of military support to ES&CI restoration in joint operations. This handbook should be treated as a guide and not as a template. It is important to understand the dynamic nature of interagency coordination and not it as step-by-step "how-to" manual. **Commanders should consider the potential benefits and risks of using this information in actual operations**.

6. Distribution and Contact Information

a. Distribution of this handbook to US Government Agencies and their Contractors is authorized. Other requests for this document shall be submitted to USJFCOM, Joint Concept Development and Experimentation, Attn: Maj Arnold Baldoza, 115 Lake View Parkway, Suffolk, VA 23435-2697; or by phone to Maj Arnold Baldoza at 757-203-3698.

b. CComments and suggestions on this important topic are welcomed. The USJFCOM JWFC points of contact are Lt Col Jeffrey Martin, 757-203-6871, jeffrey.martin@jfcom.mil; and Mr. Richard Maltz, 757-203-5553, richard.maltz.ctr@jfcom.mil.

DAN W. DAVENPORT
Rear Admiral, U.S. Navy
Director, Joint Concept Development
& Experimentation, J9

STEPHEN R. LAYFIELD
Major General, U.S. Army
Director, J7/Joint Warfighting Center

Intentionally Blank

TABLE OF CONTENTS

GLOSSARY

FIGURES

CHAPTER I
SCOPE AND INTENT

1. Overview

a. This handbook is designed to aid joint force staff members as they design, plan, and prepare for joint operations to assist a host nation (HN) in providing or restoring essential services and critical infrastructure (ES&CI) to a civilian population. Working with the ethos, "*First, do no harm*,"[2] the handbook emphasizes that the military design and plan should be crafted in such a way as to lay the foundation for, and enhance the effectiveness of follow-on local, HN, coalition, or United States Government (USG) or other civil organizations' development plans. The most effective way to meet this goal is to establish and support partnerships with the affected chief of mission (COM) and embassy country teams, the United States Agency for International Development (USAID), and other USG and international organizations who may already be, or have been engaged in such functions; to include interfacing with local, HN, coalition, and other cognizant officials and who likely will remain after US military forces depart.

b. It is important to emphasize that creating or repairing infrastructure per se' is not the goal, except when that is essential in order to save lives. The ultimate goal is to assist the HN to set up the means for the provision of fundamental government services to a target population, with a view toward long-term sustainability of the project or sector involved. The importance of this approach and these projects cannot be overstated. As they are planned and come on line, service and infrastructure projects will have a direct impact on grass-roots entrepreneurship, the overall economy, and people's daily lives. This handbook will describe, in practical terms, the nature and range of the situations that may be encountered, the types of essential services likely to be needed, the critical infrastructure systems necessary to support delivery, the needed regulatory and financial environment, issues of governance, infrastructure prioritization requirements, and the stakeholders most likely to be responsible for operating and maintaining critical infrastructures.

c. Information and recommendations in this handbook are drawn from consultations both with professionals in the infrastructure sector and military planners who have been faced with unanticipated support requirements for establishment, delivery, and maintenance of essential services to a civilian population. The bibliography lists books, articles, reports, and monographs that address the principles and procedures outlined in this handbook.

d. The principles and guidance described herein are applicable not only in post-conflict situations following combat from major interventions[3] or civil wars,[4] but also in the wake of natural disasters or as interventions in the failing or failed states during steady-state or joint operation/campaign plan Phase 0, "Shaping," operations. ES&CI restoration has occurred in countries either where there is no American Embassy (AMEMB) presence, or where the AMEMB staff was evacuated or drawn down to minimum presence. Steady-state or Phase 0 operations normally occur in countries that have an existing and often active US presence.[5] Design and planning requirements are distinctly different in the two situations. Design and planning for responses associated with a lack of US presence are done prior to the intervention using assumptions with limited in-country analysis, and then updated significantly once in-country operations begin. By contrast, design and planning for new initiatives in countries with US presence are done with significant problem identification and analysis in-country with significant input from US Embassy staff.

e. Following major interventions, the human needs of the local population must be satisfied according to their urgency and importance. The first needs that must be addressed are invariably: physical security and safety, basic sustenance, and a credible path toward prosperity/a better life (in that order). To provide these, and other pressing needs, infrastructure restoration or (re)construction is generally a major priority. Restoring public health facilities and potable water are commonly urgent requirements.[6] A good example of this is a decision reached by the US President and the UK Prime Minister to launch a joint US-UK Civil Planning Mission to Sarajevo as the top priority following North Atlantic Treaty Organization (NATO) action forcing the Serbs to stop shelling Sarajevo in 1994. Restoring electric power was identified as a top priority for Iraq following large-scale combat in 2003. Rebuilding the principal roads in Afghanistan was determined to be a priority for recovery following the fall of Taliban rule.

f. On the other hand, steady-state or Phase 0 infrastructure planning often is not a top priority, but remains an important ingredient needed to mitigate an existing or an impending crisis. Such planning must be done very carefully to assure the HN government and populations are, or will be, able to sustain the initial efforts. It requires a much greater analysis of the costs of the construction and the maintenance as well as thorough assessment of the management and technical capabilities of those responsible for ongoing maintenance, including the training requirements. Further, policy reform is often required as countries move from authoritarian, centrally-planned economies to free market economies; and governance requirements for privatization, promoting private enterprise, and streamlining the government approval processes to facilitate must be integrated into infrastructure planning.[7] Building education and health facilities; road, bridge, and pipeline construction; and water projects often are most easily identifiable because they have clear and finite objectives.

NOTE: *Planners will face strong pressure for immediate results, many requirements will appear urgent, but can ultimately detract from developing more permanent solutions. In virtually all circumstances, the military planners' ultimate goal, in close coordination with USG civilian agency partners, should include setting viable conditions for transition of responsibility to the HN both for the services and for managing the supporting infrastructure.*

g. Most military planners are neither trained nor conversant in corporate governance and economic issues, among others addressed in this handbook. This handbook is designed, however, to provide sufficient detail for a viable planning and management baseline for the civilian implementing experts who will eventually execute on the foundations laid by the joint operation plan. Whenever possible, specific planning considerations are offered as starting points for planners to address the services, infrastructure, and business climate issues they may face.

2. Key United States Government Stakeholders

The two most important civilian agency relationships in the context of this mission will be the AMEMB country team from the affected country and the USAID Office of Economic Growth and Trade (EGAT) and the Office of Infrastructure and Engineering in addition to USAID's Office of Military Affairs. The State Department Office of the Coordinator for Reconstruction and Stabilization (S/CRS) will act as a key coordinator between USG agencies (see Chapter II for details on the role of S/CRS). Contracting issues can be addressed by either USAID officers or US Army Corps of Engineers (USACE). The nongovernmental organizations (NGOs) normally can be contacted through USAID.

Intentionally Blank

CHAPTER II
SITUATION ANALYSIS

1. General

a. This chapter will examine ES&CI requirements in various situations, and provide general guidance on how these may be integrated into an overall situational analysis. Effective responses to intervention scenarios require a comprehensive interagency and multi-sectoral situational assessment, which begins with a military mission analysis. In the USG civilian community, this will be accomplished through the Interagency Conflict Analysis Framework (ICAF), which is discussed in more detail in subparagraph 3b below. The desired outcome may range from the simplest (e.g., restoring the situation to normal conditions after a major natural disaster or a failed coup d'état) in states with capable governments to a major post-conflict stabilization and reconstruction effort (e.g., for peace building or joint operation/campaign Phases IV, "Stabilize," and V, "Enable Civil Authority").

b. With an eye to enhancing HN capabilities for handling internal crises on its own, greater emphasis today is being devoted during initial analysis to carefully assess and frame (establish the context of) the problem with the aim of achieving greater effectiveness, efficiency, and economy in crisis resolution. This is part of a process called "design" or "operational design" by military planners. *In the final analysis, however, it remains the responsibility of HN authorities and civil society leaders to develop the capacity to manage their affairs effectively.* USG interventions can provide the tools and the "breathing space" necessary to institute reforms and repairs, but ultimate responsibility remains with the HN.

2. The Military Problem

How does the joint force commander (JFC) and staff design and execute ES&CI support compatible with potentially varying degrees of crisis and levels of USG intervention?

a. Potential military missions include:

    (1) Assisting in natural disaster relief efforts.

    (2) Intervention into deteriorating political conditions.

    (3) Direct intervention in post civil war situations.

    (4) Low visibility, but operationally intense, antiterrorism or counterinsurgency.

    (5) Steady state or Phase 0 operations in support of weakened economies.

b. Insurgent and terrorist organizations often exploit a weakened government by providing significant essential services designed to create legitimacy and gain popular support for their efforts. These services can rival or surpass those of the HN government or major international donor organizations. Insurgent forces generally do not have the resources to actually restore or build supporting critical infrastructure. They often forcibly appropriate this from legitimate authorities. To the extent that winning popular support is an important part of the intervention mission strategy, restoring ES&CI in support of the recognized government will be a high priority.

ANALYSIS NOTE: DEVELOPMENT PER SE MAY NOT BE A CURE

One important constraint should be noted regarding the value and contribution of development assistance programs to resolving the causes of crises. Insurgents or opposition groups that choose violent extremism may not be motivated by underlying conditions, but by ideological orientation. When the rhetoric of many of these movements is examined, the lack of references to underlying social and economic conditions is striking. Spokespersons for these movements typically appear to be more concerned with issues of identity, existential threats, perceived humiliation, cultural domination and oppression. They are generally not driven, as many social and economic root causes explanations suggest, by resentment at their inability, or the inability of their communities, to take advantage of what globalization and modernity have to offer. They often reject modernity, and harbor a fundamental hostility toward globalization and western values.

---

c. The capability of the US military to use its comparative advantage as the USG's leading expeditionary force, with its planning and operational capabilities, will be critical to mission achievement. Planners will likely have the opportunity to organize sectoral assessments as part of their comprehensive situational assessment. Humanitarian assessments, conducted by USAID Disaster Assistance Response Teams (DART), are often the first available; and usually include essential services requirements for disaster mitigation and minimizing mortality. Governance, economic, and security assessments are also conducted, although often not well-coordinated. Infrastructure assessments per se' have generally been ad hoc and poorly integrated into a comprehensive interagency situational assessment. This is a situation military planners are well-positioned to correct. Effective analysis cannot be a one-time snapshot, but must be a process repeated throughout a joint operation/campaign and regularly updated with new assessments.

3. Define the Nature of Crisis

a. Natural Disaster and Humanitarian Assistance (HA)

(1) The HA assessment will focus on saving lives and reducing suffering of the at-risk populations. Top HA priorities are to assure that the at-risk populations have physical security, food, water, shelter, and basic health services. It should be noted, however, that the provision of physical security is not generally a task for civilian HA organizations.

(2) The major categories of natural disasters are earthquakes, hurricanes, tsunamis, droughts, and floods, which often create conditions that overwhelm local capacity to respond. The first requirement is to determine how quickly minimum essential

HA needs can be restored, specifically getting the information needed to develop the design and plans to meet minimum security, water, transportation, health, and shelter requirements. It is sometimes possible, but not necessary, to include estimates of permanent infrastructure restoration requirements during the first assessment phase (see paragraph 6, "Establish a Time Horizon," below).

(3) HA efforts by the USAID Office of Foreign Disaster Assistance (OFDA), multiple NGOs, and other civilian organizations are well defined and provide temporary help to populations at risk in the immediate aftermath of a natural disaster; assuming responders have access to affected areas. Lack of access may mean providing assistance to repair roads, bridges, and landing zones to open access and support HN authorities and HA organizations in providing needed services. The objective is to stabilize affected populations, permitting them to survive at or near their home or in temporary locations, pending their return home. One desired outcome of HA effort is to facilitate the safe return of affected populations to their homes as soon as conditions permit.

(4) Donor and HN resources are seldom sufficient to reconstruct all damaged infrastructure. A "Recovery Investment Plan" developed to the extent possible with host country authorities will integrate the infrastructure requirements with economic, political, and security requirements; establishing priorities and mechanisms by which donor resources can be integrated with local resources for the most effective reconstruction effort.

SECOND-ORDER EFFECTS OF HUMANITARIAN ASSISTANCE

It is important to consider potential unintended effects of any intervention. Major immediate and longer term recovery and/or assistance efforts, required in the aftermath of catastrophic natural disaster, where perhaps hundreds of thousands of people have been placed at risk, can be expected to have dramatic impact beyond reestablishing basic services and infrastructure. When such disasters occur in countries challenged by weak political or economic structures, where civil unrest can be provoked or already exists, the impact of intervention can have significant political or other implications. Whenever actions are taken in a complex environment to change a condition, state, or paradigm, the "Law of Unintended Consequences" is almost invariably invoked. These consequences can have far-reaching and randomly distributed effects, for good and ill. Managing those effects will be a key function of HA. An example of this was in Aceh, Indonesia, where the heaviest damage from the 2004 Indian Ocean tsunami occurred, a years-long insurrection against the government had been underway. The massive international response to the humanitarian crisis and influx of global investment and scrutiny provided the catalyst for the government and the insurgents to hold talks toward resolving their conflict. Careful analysis, and consideration of possible effects, can avoid unplanned negative results and may provide an otherwise unanticipated opportunity to promote desired outcomes.

b. **Political-Military Intervention and Civil War**

(1) Whereas natural disasters requiring international assistance occur frequently, the larger challenges have proven to be major interventions triggered by civil

war, abusive governments, genocide, insurrection, or cross-border invasion. For some interventions, such as Bosnia in 1995, force-on-force combat is not required and ES&CI restoration can focus directly on damage done by warring factions prior to the intervention.[8] The Kosovo intervention required aerial bombardment, but it was directed against an abusive government in its own territory, so reconstruction assistance was not required in Serbia proper. The two combat interventions in Iraq and the one in Afghanistan had regime change as a principal objective, thus re-establishment of ES&CI were major requirements of support for the new governments being established. Other interventions that do not require combat (e.g., Somalia in 1991, Haiti and Rwanda in 1994) may still have important infrastructure requirements (e.g., transportation infrastructure for food delivery in Somalia, potable water supply in Rwanda).

(2) Civil wars such as those in Liberia, Sierra Leone, Somalia, and the former Yugoslavia can be devastating. Although USG and international intervention in active civil wars cannot be assumed; by the end of such wars, the warring governments are nearly always devoid of resources, and therefore dependent on international assistance.

(3) As noted earlier, restoration of ES&CI to support new governments in the case of regime change following destructive interventions can be critical as a means for these new governments to gain the respect of their populations. This has been demonstrated recently in Afghanistan and Iraq. The significant cost of infrastructure reconstruction requires a significant design and planning effort to most effectively use the resources available, and to integrate the infrastructure reconstruction strategy into the HN's economic, political, and security strategy. Every attempt must be made to assure that reconstruction and stabilization activities are seen by the locals as new government initiatives or, more reasonably, as new government-led collaborations with intervening forces. The most cost-effective and politically expedient assistance in new government establishment will be those actions that restore stability as quickly as possible, help it put its new policies in place, and build its capacity to manage new institutions. Effective management of reconstruction activities can, in turn, be an important training ground to build effective governance. **Thus, assessing the mid- and long-term requirements simultaneously with the immediate requirements contributes to a cost-effective, long-term reconstruction program**.

(4). The level of resources provided by the US and the international donor community can vary considerably. The level of commitment reflects varying political considerations of those donors. Insofar as is possible, coordinated planning for the effective use of available resources should be a primary consideration. Further, in a post-civil war environment, the capability of the HN to effectively manage its economy becomes an important factor in design and planning; particularly since some donors, such as the World Bank, provide reconstruction assistance only as loans that must be repaid.

c. Insurgency and Terrorism

(1) Insurgencies are similar to civil wars, but are generally less intense and more protracted. They occur in countries with viable and functioning governments that can usually maintain their essential services and reconstruct their critical infrastructure when damaged. Latin America and Caribbean insurgencies are the best-known examples

in recent times. **The nature of ES&CI efforts under an insurgency will generally be in support of HN institutional efforts.** Insurgent attacks are both difficult to anticipate and, by design, focus on interrupting political and economic activities. As such, planning for reconstruction is difficult, and is based on projections of the most likely damages that might be inflicted. The provision of physical security by the HN, augmented as necessary by external forces, is a necessary element to enabling an effective ES&CI restoration effort.

(2) Terrorism is a common tactic in insurgency and civil war that nurtures fear to influence public (and sometimes official) support for or against policies of interest to the terrorist(s). Infrastructure is often targeted to create fear and to disrupt government services. Antiterrorism security measures may include infrastructure hardening and other construction to protect facilities, population groups, and/or government buildings to reduce the effectiveness of terrorist attacks. An important planning factor may be to work to minimize the flexibility of terrorist leaders to adjust to protective measures that are taken. Accordingly, the potential cost-effectiveness of such infrastructure security measures becomes an important factor in planning.

NOTE: *For most of today's military operations, simply returning to a pre intervention status will only restore the conditions that originally led to the crisis, and may therefore be inappropriate as a mission objective. Mission analysis needs to identify where restorations or enhancements to pre existing systems can ultimately negate or mitigate the nominal cause of a crisis situation.*

d. Weak Economy: Phase 0 Operations

(1) Under recent DOD guidance, military commands are to increase the priority given to designing, planning, and conducting activities in countries prior to the occurrence of a crisis, with the intention of preventing or mitigating the crisis.[9] This guidance significantly increases the attention given to building partner nation capacity during Phase 0, or steady-state, periods. DOS and USAID have established similar policies for working in "fragile" states (states moving toward, in, or emerging from crises). Designing and planning activities in these states are performed very differently than in situations above, where the crisis has already occurred.

(2) For example, **in a state with a functioning, sovereign government, and where no government change is intended, the established government must not only be a willing participant, but must be seen as a leader in intervention, design, planning, and operations management.** Its disposition to both acknowledge a pending crisis and agree that action is warranted is critical, and cannot be assumed. This is often politically difficult for HN governments, because the admission may signal it is losing, or has lost control of, conditions in the country. Phase 0 design, planning, and operations must be conducted with the greatest sensitivity and respect to HN policies and programs. Every effort must be made, during implementation, to project a supporting rather than a leadership role, and to achieve the effect of bolstering confidence in the host government.

(3) Other positive differences include a much reduced sense of urgency, which will permit a more systematic approach and much wider interest in, and participation

by, bilateral and international organizations in the crisis resolution effort. Restoration of essential services and rebuilding critical infrastructure *per se'* normally should not be the primary objective. Rather, the focus should be on sustaining and improving existing HN services and systems. Since the trigger of a possible crisis is very difficult to predict, anticipation is primarily an exercise in judgment. Given the lack of a proximate crisis, allocation of significant resources to planning or preparation may be difficult to justify.

(4) Measuring and sustaining the capacity of a host government to perform essential services and to maintain and build critical infrastructure is a simpler task if the work can be done incrementally. This is far better than attempting to rebuild and restore significantly damaged services and infrastructure rapidly and under crisis conditions.

(5) A critical factor in Phase 0 design and planning for ES&CI restoration is determining how the HN will sustain completed projects.[10] Installation of generators, for example, will have little effect on available electricity if provision for operation and maintenance, such as training, spare parts, and repair is not considered. This becomes, in large measure, an exercise in expectation management for both the donor and the HN. New school and hospital buildings can not achieve their desired effect without teachers, doctors, equipment, staff, and maintenance capability for sanitary water facilities, etc. Failures in this regard are symptomatic of inadequate public policy planning (i.e., health services probably require actions from the ministry of finance, not just the ministry of health).

(6) Planners must also anticipate that cultural differences may create unanticipated challenges. For example, that host country military policies, practices, and procedures may not be disposed to operate in an expected manner, or be accountable to the populations, or even include considerations of the public welfare. In such cases, planners may need to focus first on policy reform options that respect cultural mores, and recognize that new practices and procedures will need to be reasonably acceptable to the governed. Chapter III addresses sectoral policy issues in some detail.

4. Framing the Problem

a. **Scope of the Effort.** The wide range of ES&CI restoration situations encountered during Phase 0 and post-conflict, Phases IV and V, requires a careful formulation of activities. In general, most interventions should begin with the assumption that reconstruction and stabilization activities will act to support HN governance, whether already existing or emerging after the intervention. The following categories illustrate the possibilities:

(1) **Straightforward technical/engineering planning, design and implementation unencumbered by socio-political concerns**. This can happen if the socio-economic concerns are considered minimal; or if the program managers outside the military have taken that responsibility and coordinated the broader issues with the military.

(2) **ES&CI restoration activities solely oriented toward a defined local geographic area(s)**, where the activities do not have national scale or broader considerations. A situational analysis of the local socio-economic considerations is usually needed to assure that the activities are appropriate and sustainable.

(3) **Rapid response requirements**, such as responding to natural disasters or the immediate aftermath of a conflict, **to save lives and reduce suffer**ing. Socio-economic issues are generally immediately apparent and early action can not wait for comprehensive assessments. Some rapid-response assessment will be needed, however, to assure appropriately directed action.

(4) **Operations under HN authority**. HN authorities remain in charge, have a limited capability, and have requested specific actions to support stabilization or crisis response conditions. Close coordination here reduces the chances for inappropriate actions. A limited situational analysis with HN authorities is still appropriate, however, to assure that HN authorities have adequately covered their own socio-economic considerations.

(5) **A major intervention with a change in governance** that will require a complete range of assessments and a comprehensive situational analysis with continual updates.

b. **Interagency Assessments: Aligning with Country Reconstruction and Stabilization Group (CRSG) Policy Decisions**

(1) A 2005 Presidential Decision, National Security Presidential Directive 44 (NSPD-44), led to the establishment within the S/CRS. This office's responsibility is to coordinate interagency responses to major crises. S/CRS established the Interagency Management System (IMS)[11] to help mange the interagency planning process. Primary elements of the process include:

(a) **CRSG** – A Washington-based interagency decision-making body.

(b) **Advance Civilian Team (ACT)** – Field teams to deploy to crisis countries to assist with AMEMB country team planning.

(c) **Integration Planning Cell (IPC)** – A team to deploy to geographic combatant commands to assist with crisis action planning.

(d) **USG Planning Framework** – Planning guidance to use for the development of strategic plans for specific crises.

(2) In the course of an intervention, joint forces will generally be operating under the guidance of the CRSG for operations related to stabilization and reconstruction. The CRSG will set the policy and strategy directions that will be passed through Office of the Secretary of Defense and the Joint Staff to the joint operation/campaign planners. It is intended that, through these new institutional practices, interventions will be as effective, efficient, and economical as possible. The USG further intends to integrate civilian-oriented stability and reconstruction into joint operation design and planning, in order to assure the most effective transition from combat to stability operations. A detailed review of military participation in the IMS is discussed in the *Commander's Handbook for Military Participation in the Interagency Management System*, which is Book 1 of this sectoral handbook series.

(3) As part of the USG *Planning Framework and Practitioners Guide*, preparations for an intervention will include a situational assessment. At the strategic and political level, a key component of this will be an analysis of the conflict's causes and manifestations using the ICAF.[12] Other sectoral assessments, such as *Measuring Progress in Conflict Environments* (MPICE)[13], to the extent available, also will contribute to the overall situational assessment (e.g., HA, governance, economic, etc.) The MPICE is discussed in greater detail in Chapter IV of this handbook.

(4) The importance of submitting carefully-prepared recommendations to senior officials needs to be stressed. The reason for this is well-stated in United States Army Training and Doctrine Command's (TRADOC's) Commander's Appreciation and Campaign Design (CACD) pamphlet as follows:

> *"CACD recognizes that orders flow from higher to lower, but understanding often flows from lower to higher, especially when operational problems are complex. In these cases, a commander is often in a better position than his superiors to understand the full scope of a complex operational problem. Thus it is more likely that commanders at all levels will frame the problem themselves and then share their understanding with their superiors and subordinates. . . . A significant goal of CACD is a shared understanding of complex problems. This requires battlefield circulation by higher commanders; candid discourse with superiors, subordinates, peers and staff; and strategic thinking at all levels."*[14]

c. **Mission Objectives**

(1) Military planners will need to know and incorporate or accommodate civilian interests and requirements in joint operation/campaign design and planning. For steady-state Phase 0 operations, military planners should consult the AMEMB's, *Mission Strategic Plan*, and USAID's, *Country Assistance Strategy*, that provide guidance to comprehensive USG operations. S/CRS plans include drafting a pre-deployment interagency strategic plan to be followed by a significant revision by the interagency planning team after deployment. This strategic plan is based on a situational assessment that includes a set of critical key assumptions; including the general conditions that are anticipated such as the host government status and nature of its cooperation, extent of ES&CI damage, number of at-risk populations, security conditions, and the latent capacity of the HN to restore its economy. These assumptions must be revised constantly, based on evolving conditions. As mentioned previously, a critical element is the provision of adequate security which will allow for the effective conduct of activities to assist the HN restore ES&CI.

(2) Military plans include lines of operations (LOOs), with tasks and sub-tasks. The S/CRS's strategic plan equivalent is main mission elements (MMEs), with objectives and tasks. The full plan may be found in the *United States Government Draft Planning Framework for Reconstruction, Stabilization, and Conflict Transformation: Practitioner's Guide, November 2008 Version*. It also is discussed in detail in Book 1 of this handbook series, *Military Participation in the Interagency Management System*.

MISSION OBJECTIVES (EXAMPLE)

The overall mission objective is usually generic, as evidenced by the published Coalition Provisional Authority (CPA) goal for Iraq:

"The ultimate goal is a unified and stable, democratic Iraq that: provides effective and representative government for the Iraqi people; is underpinned by new and protected freedoms for all Iraqis and a growing market economy; is able to defend itself but no longer poses a threat to its neighbors or international security."[15]

The CPA MMEs for Iraq were security, essential services, economy, governance, and strategic communication. The end state for essential services in the CPA Strategic Plan was:

"Essential services and infrastructure, including particularly electricity, water and health care, are provided to acceptable standards that at least match pre-war provision. Plans are in place, and where feasible being implemented, to improve the quality, and accessibility by all citizens, of all public services."[16]

Note: The Tasks, and particularly the sub-tasks, under the lines of effort and MMEs, must be written to reflect specific outcomes within specific time periods. The standard criteria of writing objectives apply; they must be: measurable, worthwhile, realistic, achievable, sustainable and resourced. Shown here are selected examples of tasks and sub-tasks included in the "CPA Strategic Plan Essential Services" section:

"Provide electricity services that meet national needs.

- *Improve generating capacity to 6,000 Megawatts (from 3200-3500 in July '03) by 1 July, 04.*

- *Fully implement policy on allocation of electrical power, through fair load shedding 3 hrs on/3 hrs off for domestic and commercial consumers.*

Reconstruct communications and postal systems and introduce advanced technologies.

- *Restore fixed phone capabilities to pre-war levels.*

- *Establish mobile wireless service in three regions.*

- *Establish comprehensive communications regulatory framework.*

Provide food security for all Iraqis."[17]

d. Infrastructure-Specific Assessments: ES&CI Restoration Roles and Priorities

(1) Restoration of essential services and reconstruction of critical infrastructure can often be a straightforward technical task. This is the case when political issues following a crisis are minimal. Not surprisingly, however, most recent experiences have not been that simple.

> The Sarajevo example is one example of a comprehensive assessment. It was based on the United Nations Security Council Resolution 900, and was tasked with determining the needs of highest priority. It was conducted March 8-23, 1994. A summary of the results is the following, stating the estimates in Deutsche Marks – DM (note that this assessment divided the estimates into near-term and longer-term requirements):
>
> | Sector | Repair/Rehabilitation | Transitional Program |
> |---|---|---|
> | Electric Power | 31,400,000 DM | 104,850,000 DM |
> | Water Supply/Sanitation | 69,000,000 DM | 27,300,000 DM |
> | Solid Waste Collection | 960,000 DM | 8,910,000 DM |
> | Gas | 13,330,000 DM | 17,370,000 DM |
> | Health | 7,210,000 DM | 4,170,000 DM |
> | City Transportation | 18,150,000 DM | 42,000,000 DM |
> | Road/Rail Transportation | | 13,600,000 DM |
> | Central Heating | 1,650,000 DM | 10,000,000 DM |
> | Production Enterprises | | 10,000,000 DM |
> | Telecommunications | 20,000,000 DM | 400,000 DM |
> | Education | | 10,000,000 DM |
> | Housing | 28,000,000 DM | 900,000 DM |
> | Other | | 3,960,000 DM |
>
> The estimates for each of the sectors are summaries of the specific project activities examined. This team included several experts with prior experience in Bosnia.[18]

(2) If infrastructure requirements are large, and significant funding is made available for reconstruction, the requirement for accountability becomes a priority, often neglected in the pressure to achieve objectives that tend to be accelerated for reasons of expediency. This, in turn, leads to the need to establish institutional management and regulatory structures within the HN government to assure that financial management is effective. Thus, it becomes incumbent on planners to understand the broader implications of reconstruction operations, include them in the plan, and ensure that top leadership understands the importance of management, as well as the technical plans. These issues are discussed in more detail in Chapter III.

e. **Assessment Mechanics and Baseline Assessments.** Various types of specific infrastructure-specific assessments can be conducted, depending on the situation (see subparagraph 4a, "Scope of the Effort," above). The guidance below expands on the scoping problem by looking at two specific methods for conducting assessments:

(1) **Using the Defense Critical Infrastructure Program (DCIP) as a Model for Setting a Baseline Assessment**. The DCIP is a DOD program designed to provide centralized assessment and management of critical infrastructure systems that support the DOD mission. Although its operational emphasis is on supporting infrastructure in a fully-developed, CONUS-like environment, the DCIP assessment process is adaptable to intervention scenarios where planners need to create a comprehensive review of existing conditions before designing and planning the restoration and/or establishment of supporting infrastructure. Sectors examined by this program include: **energy** (electrical, natural gas, and petroleum), **industrial chemical** (storage and use), **communications** (electrical voice and data transmission), **transportation** (aviation, road and highway, rail, and maritime), **water** (potable, industrial, firefighting, and wastewater), **supporting utilities** (heating, ventilation, and air conditioning [HVAC]), and **enabling assets**. The full program may be found in the DOD Instruction 3020.45 series. For the specific sectors highlighted by **bold text** above, their assessment benchmark questionnaires are included in Appendix B of this handbook.

(2) **Continuous Assessment**. It is important to stress that, for situations like Iraq and Afghanistan, where conflict continues simultaneously with reconstruction, assessment is a continuous process rather than a single snapshot of the situation. As changes occur, they can lead to substantial alterations of priorities, and even of policy and strategy. In particular, when inconsistencies in accountability of infrastructure construction are detected, it is important to raise that to the attention of senior reconstruction managers. The evolution of passing authority to the host government for reconstruction management requires constant attention. For example, the desire of the USG to have the Palestinian Authority lead Gaza reconstruction efforts following the January 2009 conflict demonstrates the political importance of performing infrastructure reconstruction effectively.

5. Prioritization of Key Services and Infrastructure

a. General

(1) The primary focus for essential services during initial responses to crises are the core HA criteria – saving lives and reducing suffering. Once those are realized, attention can be given to longer-term ES&CI restoration activities. One frequent complication is that at-risk populations may be refugees or internally-displaced persons (IDPs).[19] An important HA objective is to take refugees and IDPs back to their homes as quickly as practicable. No permanent infrastructure is constructed for refugee or IDP camps for that reason. Only if it is determined that these populations are unable to return home for political reasons, is permanent infrastructure constructed for long-term occupancy.

(2) Perhaps the most challenging requirement for large operations is to conduct an infrastructure design and planning process that determines the priorities and sequencing of critical infrastructure construction based on the broader strategic plan priorities and resources availability. The technical expertise available and used for infrastructure planning and operations likely also will be of value to the reconstruction planning team. Gantt chart information systems software can be immensely valuable to field planners

and managers, not just for infrastructure projects but to integrate infrastructure project plans with the other related response activities. The discussion below provides examples of when each of the various infrastructure requirements became a priority. Competition for priority designation is common in the wake of combat or a natural disaster; and using information technology systems can increase effectiveness in decision making. Figure II-1 illustrates the results of a hypothetical "MS Project" chart that illustrates the relationship and sequencing among nominal infrastructure, governance, and other development projects.

(3) Gaining back public confidence in the government of a country dependent on hydroelectric power for both domestic use and export (e.g., Laos) following a conflict, requires restoration of hydroelectric power production. Reconstruction can begin only after a legitimate government is established and regulatory measures are in place. Thus in Figure II-1, the critical path, shown in red, passes through multiple lines of operation.

b. **Sector-Specific Considerations**. Each essential service can become a priority based on the circumstances and analysis of the situation. Key priorities would commonly include:

(1) **Potable Water and Food**

(a) Water is always a priority to sustain life. It is especially a requirement for refugees and IDPs. Temporary water infrastructure can be important even to meet short-term requirements. During Operation PROVIDE COMFORT in northern Iraq in 1991, more than 400,000 Kurds fled to the mountains bordering Turkey where potable water was unavailable to sizeable population groups and they were not permitted to cross into Turkey. The NGO, International Rescue Committee, sent a technician who found the limited water sources available and piped water to the IDP locations. In developing plans to establish an IDP camp at a site down from the mountains, two criteria were used to select the site: a) near a town/city where water facilities were available (i.e., Zakho), and; b) a location which had water (i.e., a spring). A water pumping system was installed and a water tower was erected to provide water to the IDPs brought into the site.

(b) One constraint which will likely be common in water supply systems in crisis states is the imperfect state of the water distribution system. This was an important problem in Sarajevo – significant quantities of water were lost due to leakage in the city system which had not been well-maintained.

THE SARAJEVO SIEGE

The Sarajevo siege in 1992-4 resulted in water facilities being cut off from the residents by the Serbs who controlled the water pumping stations outside the city. Although the UN crisis managers negotiated restoration of water service, the non-resolution of the conflict caused constant interruptions. Sarajevo did have a small river running through it, but that water was not considered potable and the Bosniacs feared that the water may well be intentionally polluted. An NGO, working with United Nations protection force (UNPROFOR) and the United Nations Office of the High Commission for Refugees (UNHCR), imported generator purification sets to purify river water and insert it into the city water system.

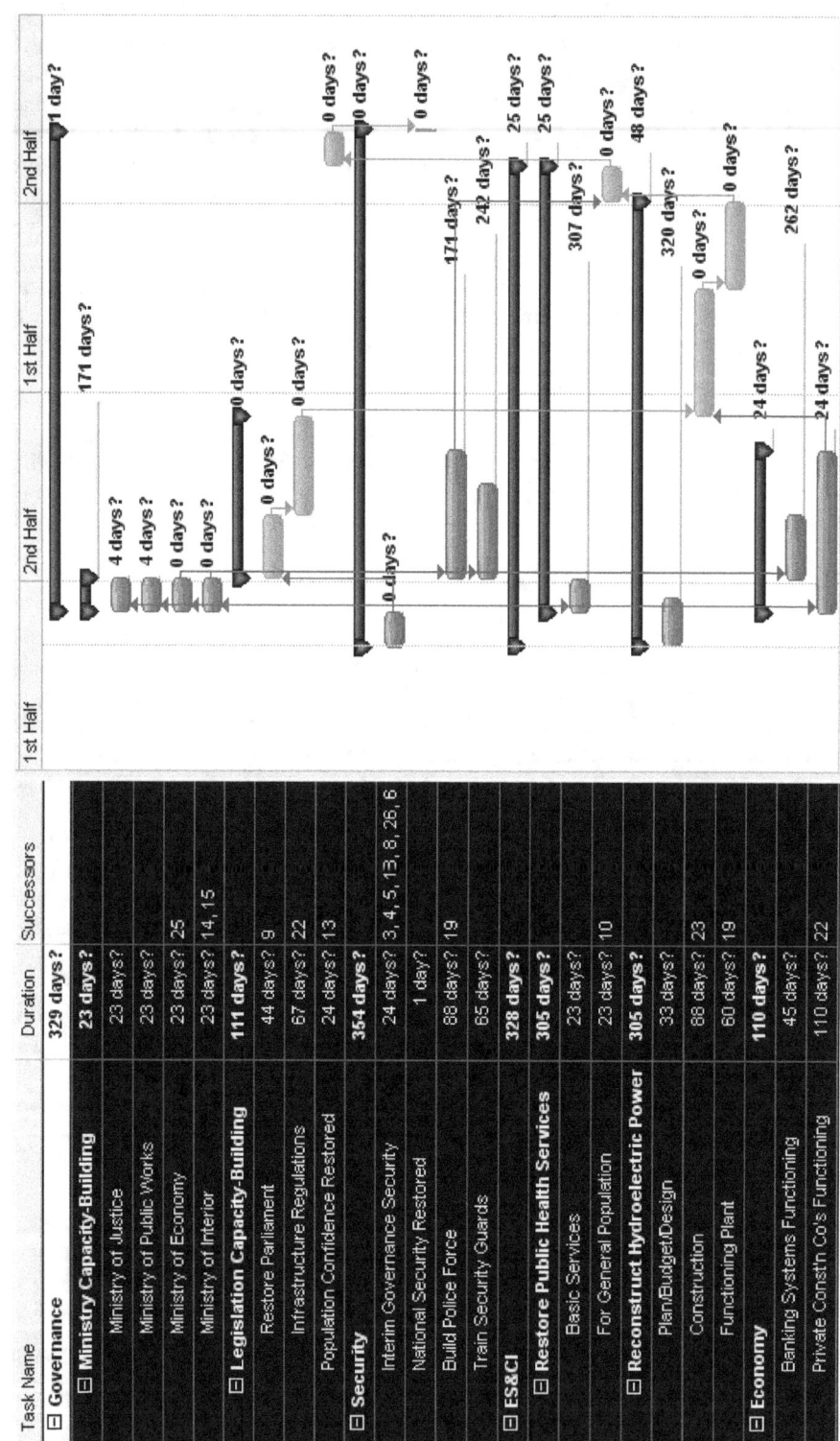

Figure II-1. Critical Path Through Multiple Lines of Operations

Task Name	Duration	Successors
⊟ **Governance**	**329 days?**	
⊟ **Ministry Capacity-Building**	**23 days?**	
Ministry of Justice	23 days?	
Ministry of Public Works	23 days?	
Ministry of Economy	23 days?	25
Ministry of Interior	23 days?	14, 15
⊟ **Legislation Capacity-Building**	**111 days?**	
Restore Parliament	44 days?	9
Infrastructure Regulations	67 days?	22
Population Confidence Restored	24 days?	13
⊟ **Security**	**354 days?**	
Interim Governance Security	24 days?	3, 4, 5, 13, 8, 26, 6
National Security Restored	1 day?	
Build Police Force	88 days?	19
Train Security Guards	65 days?	
⊟ **ES&CI**	**328 days?**	
⊟ **Restore Public Health Services**	**305 days?**	
Basic Services	23 days?	
For General Population	23 days?	10
⊟ **Reconstruct Hydroelectric Power**	**305 days?**	
Plan/Budget/Design	33 days?	
Construction	88 days?	23
Functioning Plant	60 days?	19
⊟ **Economy**	**110 days?**	
Banking Systems Functioning	45 days?	
Private Constr'n Co's Functioning	110 days?	22

II-13

(c) Rebuilding or restoring water facilities as part of long-term reconstruction efforts is usually necessary. The repetitive civil wars in Liberia required a periodic restoration of its primary water supply facility. The Baghdad water supply facilities were high on the list for restoration after the 2003 intervention. Restoring water systems is also constrained by the availability of electric power to drive the pumps, an interrelationship that raised the priority in restoring electrical power in Baghdad.

(d) During steady-state Phase 0 operations, well-drilling or well-digging is a popular activity for communities lacking easy access to potable water. In addition to knowing water table accessibility, two constraints need to be examined in an assessment: does the community have the capacity to maintain a pump that is installed or to public works maintenance services, and are there any environmental considerations (i.e., aquifer depletion, waste water flow). Attention must also be paid to the tensions and linkages between water as a life resource and water as part of a sanitation system.

(e) Food assistance is generally provided under HA efforts managed by USAID's OFDA and by international organizations such as the World Food Program, UNICEF, and the International Red Cross. OFDA will send to the field DARTs to assess and provide funding to NGOs to administer food aid programs. DART teams have, in the past, frequently worked alongside military units in crisis response operations, including being embedded with these units.

(f) For politically sensitive interventions, care is required to separate civilian and military operations, once civilians are able to undertake their HA operations. NGOs often believe themselves to be, and actually might be, at risk, if they are identified as working with military units. Because of this, efforts are often required to avoid that association.

(g) On rare occasions, the military might find itself the only entity with access to at-risk populations, due to non-permissive conditions (i.e., an uncertain or hostile operational environment). To the extent it is possible, it should only provide food assistance under the guidance and instructions of DART officials who will usually accept invitations to embed with the military.

(2) **Health Services**

(a) Restoring essential emergency health services (e.g., hospital, clinic, other medical services facilities) is a high priority, especially for the short-term. Illness and injury generally accompany conflict and natural disasters. Infrastructure requirements may not be an immediate priority, however, for three reasons: 1. health facilities are often not targeted and damage to them may therefore not be extensive, 2. health services are often maintained during crises due to their importance for local populations, and 3. health services for refugees and IDPs are usually provided on-site in temporary facilities provided by health services NGOs. However, **power and water are critical for health facilities**. Providing power through generator sets or repairing the on-site back-up generators often installed at hospitals will likely be a very high priority.

(b) One important reference for health services standards is found under the "Standardized Monitoring and Assessment of Relief and Transitions Initiative." The concept, and its accompanying tools, have been widely adopted by the international humanitarian community; and adherence to it is now common among host governments, the UN, and NGOs.[20]

(c) Classic, life-saving interventions (i.e., providing oral rehydration, measles vaccination campaigns, widespread distribution of malaria bed nets, and other programs that form the core of emergency relief operations) need to be conducted. Yet none of these depend on fully functional health systems; nor, in many instances, are they the highest priority for a war-weary population. While never abandoning those activities that are the hallmarks of humanitarian action, mid-to-long term requirements need to be considered from the outset. Strong consideration should be given for starting to plan for the construction and rehabilitation of primary health care facilities (not tertiary care hospitals that only serve the needs of the wealthy or those living in urban areas). This includes planning for adequate staff and the procurement and regular distribution of drugs and supplies. By doing so, both humanitarian and political objectives can be met, and a fledgling government can become more legitimate in the eyes of a wary population.

(d) Planning and programming the transition of health sector activities from immediate to long-term reconstruction requirements need to be initiated as quickly as possible. In order to determine program priorities in the health sector, program planners have to have a deeper understanding of the complex operational problems that they will need to address, and design a broad approach to problem solving. This starts with basic HA, and continues with conducting health sector assessments. The challenge is to determine how to balance immediate service delivery needs with shorter-term actions focused on enhanced stability, and longer-term actions to build national capacity and restore a functioning health system.

(e) Appendix D contains detailed health sector planning considerations. A comprehensive review of health sector requirements may also be found in the *World Health Organization Handbook*.[21]

NOTE: *It is essential to consult with health experts as part of assessing health infrastructure requirements. The infrastructure cost and the maintenance burden for HNs is an important factor in making decisions on new construction during steady state Phase 0 operations and in reconstruction of existing facilities for post conflict responses. For example, Sarajevo maintained two full service hospitals for a pre war population of a little over 500,000. But Bosnia had few, if any, preventive health care facilities (private doctors and clinics). The assessment team, which included health experts, concluded that health sector policy reform was required prior to considering the reconstruction of the second hospital.*

(3) **Emergency Services**. Fire department and ambulance services may be proposed as an early necessity in an intervention scenario. However, they are generally considered to be part of second-order municipal services, important but not critical in the

early stages of an intervention. As with most direct support to a local community, planners must work to ensure they are not creating false expectations or unrealistic performance standards that could potentially undermine the authority of the host government.

(4) Energy Supply

(a) The importance of electrical power generation and heating facilities is dependent on the climate of the country in crisis, and the nature of its economic activity. In countries with tropical climates, it does not play an important role in the immediate requirements for saving lives and reducing suffering. However, heating during the winter in temperate climates quickly becomes a priority in order to sustain healthy conditions for the population, particularly in urban areas where heating options are limited.

SARAJEVO ENERGY CRISIS

Heating was a priority in Sarajevo during the winter months during the 1992-95 siege. Many trees were cut down, and furniture and books were used in small stoves people built for their apartments. Sarajevo was in the process of converting to natural gas supplied by Russia. One infrastructure activity during the conflict was extending the natural gas pipes to larger areas of the city, and it became a priority for post-conflict reconstruction.

(b) Electrical power generation quickly became a priority in Iraq, partly because Iraq had an economy that required electricity, and partly because of its convenience as a metric to measure progress in reconstruction. Unfortunately, electrical production had been very poorly supported in the pre-war period; and the state of the electrical production and distribution system was very poor. Significant resources were required for both restoration and building new facilities to prepare for future prosperity.

(c) Pre-deployment planning must include identifying the power generation and distribution and central heating facilities to assure they are not targeted, or that planned damage can be quickly repaired. It is unlikely that power generation and heating will be the focus of infrastructure construction during steady-state Phase 0 operations. The length of time required to achieve results, the resource requirements, and the need to support capacity development to manage these facilities all militate against engaging in this activity in a short time frame. It is possible, however, that steady-state Phase 0 activity or post-conflict Phases IV and V reconstruction of power generation facilities in limited geographic areas could be a priority for political purposes.

(5) Shelter and Housing

(a) Building refugee or IDP camps can become a priority when they can not return home quickly. The quality of the camps is a function of the speed in which they need to be built and their degree of permanency. Tents or plastic sheeting can be erected quickly for large numbers of refugees or IDPs for short-term occupation. It is always an objective to build camps as close to their original homes as possible to encourage them to return home. More permanent construction is sometimes required, but it is not a desirable solution for an intervention force. Tents and plastic sheeting can be obtained from relief organizations that stockpile these commodities. UNHCR is the pre-eminent international organization for shelter supplies.

(b) Conflict that occurs in densely populated urban centers can potentially create significant damage to apartment buildings and residences that house large numbers of people. Housing reconstruction could therefore become a high priority activity to avoid supporting long-term IDP camps. Since World War II, no events have occurred which caused extensive damage to large urban centers (population of two million or larger); so the infrastructure assessment, reconstruction planning, and implementing programs would have to be done without guidance developed from recent past experience.

(c) Government buildings and other governance facilities may also be in critical need of restoration. The deliberate destruction of ministry buildings in Baghdad caused considerable delay in restoring government activities. It is particularly important in pre-intervention planning to identify governance facilities that will be crucial in restoring government operations in the post-conflict period. As with power generators, planners should ensure that targeted facilities have appropriate repair priority.

(6) **Transportation**

(a) Repair of roads and bridges will be a top priority when access to locations with at-risk populations is limited due to damage caused by natural disasters or conflict. Assessing this requirement needs to be done with HA assessors. Hurricane Mitch (2008- Central America) is one example where transportation links suffered considerable damage; and the level of relief requirements far exceeded what could be supplied by air. The capacity of railroads, if they exist, to meet relief requirements will be part of the assessments. This is not a reason to ignore rail; however, as it has potential to permit high-volume surface transportation that may be critical to long-term economic viability. Planners should be attentive to the political ramifications of rail creation and/or restoration as it provides easy access between potentially disparate geographical regions. Ports and airports will also need to be assessed. In particular, if ports are necessary to support delivery of emergency commodities or to facilitate the restoration of economic activity, they could be a priority in reconstruction. The need for dredging of the critical port and maritime terminal at Basra in Iraq was an important early example; progress was slow, and impeding economic recovery and flows of required materials and commodities.

SARAJEVO PUBLIC TRANSPORTATION

Assessment priority for public transportation in cities will depend on its importance in restoring economic activity. For example, one of the most used public transportation facilities in Sarajevo was the streetcar system. Restoring its operations was considered a major symbol of progress by the city government, contributing to improving the morale of city residents, and renewing confidence in government.

(b) For the mid-to-long-term, road reconstruction may be a recovery priority. The Afghanistan government considered road construction a high priority in early post-conflict infrastructure recovery efforts. A major constraint to building effective governance was traditional hostility toward central government rulers by populations in outlying areas. Expanding the influence of centralized government, and integrating national economic activity, can be facilitated by having better roads. The high cost and longer times for delivery of transportation infrastructure, however, must be considered in making recommendations on undertaking transportation reconstruction activities.

(1) **Communications Services, Media, and Wireless**

(a) All ES&CI restoration experiences have placed a high priority on both restoring communications systems and assessing the opportunity for upgrading and modernizing communications infrastructures. Restoring land-line and microwave systems to revive previously existing capacities is the first step. The process of assessing requirements needs to include building an effective public-private sector partnership. This is because private sector investment generally comes more rapidly with the attractiveness of new technology. Assessing the regulatory environment is a critical part of the process to determine policy reform and new institutional requirements that must be put in place to assure an effective communications system. See Chapter III for more guidance on structuring the business environment.

(b) Media infrastructure requirements often will be a high priority, in conjunction with building effective participative governance. The host government's ability to inform the public of government activities to support public interests may be crucial to gaining popular support.

(c) Existing communications facilities pose a challenge for planners, as they are often crucial to adversaries as well. Because they are important to post-conflict governance, targeting decisions must be made with considerable judgment and care.

(d) For steady-state Phase 0 operations, both communications and media infrastructure may be considered for support if they are assessed as weaknesses for the existing host government. It is not a likely activity for a military initiative, but if combined with requirements for HN security institutions, it would rank higher on the list of possible priorities.

(e) Planners must be particularly attentive to the requirements of the modern wireless communications sector, even in regions where the advanced technology would seem to be out of place. Recent experience has shown that the commercial sector puts emphasis on creating a viable wireless network for the full range of wireless applications. Accordingly, planners must anticipate that spectrum management in particular will be an immediate commercial and economic issue, demanding a high degree of coordination between military users, and civilian partners in USAID, and the Department of Commerce, to say nothing of the host government.

(7) Education

(a) A high priority for aid donors working in prolonged conflict situations is to find ways to keep children in school. A specialized NGO has even been created that focuses on this requirement, the International Network for Education in Emergencies. It is always a priority to restore education institutions to functioning capacity early in the post-conflict period. The needs are widespread; and it is impossible to meet them all. Because provisional facilities often serve needs adequately, school reconstruction is generally not as high a priority as infrastructure requirements necessary for restoring economic activity. But local government officials often place priority on school reconstruction because of the priority given to education by their constituents. The assessment of education infrastructure requirements must include the availability of teachers and school supplies. New school construction where schools did not exist before should not be funded if teachers are not available.

(b) Repairing and building schools is one of the most popular steady-state activities. A proposal to build a school is generally acceptable and approved by the local population and authorities. It is finite, does not take a long time, and is a relatively straightforward project. However, the same assessment requirements of teacher and school materials availability are applicable as for post-conflict efforts.

(8) Agriculture

(a) Restoration of agriculture production is an absolutely necessary recovery activity. Infrastructure requirements in support of restoring agriculture production and delivery are generally neither an immediate nor a high priority. Agriculture production is usually not badly affected by conflict, unless there is a major population displacement or a deliberate scorched earth campaign. Marketing of agriculture products requires access to roads, and is examined as part of the transportation assessment. Agriculture requirements, however, should also be included in the infrastructure assessment.

(b) Any country that has extensive irrigated agriculture, like Iraq, may have infrastructure restoration requirements. Restoration may be a labor-intensive activity that also contributes to reducing unemployment, and may thus be an attractive prospect for support. The more sophisticated the agriculture production system, the closer the infrastructure restoration requirements need to be examined. Production, transportation, storage, processing, and marketing infrastructure requirements may exist. In Northern Iraq, during Operation PROVIDE COMFORT in 1991, the intervention was conducted during the wheat growing season. Harvesting was done by machine harvesters that came from outside the established secure zone. Storage was in a large silo and warehouse facility in Zakho. All this infrastructure needed to be available and in operating condition to avoid wasting wheat production.

(9) Production Enterprises

(a) Restoration of certain production enterprises is essential in support of reconstruction activities. Cement and brick-making plants, for example, supply critical construction materials. Metal working enterprises are necessary for normal economic activity. Assessments include the status of production facilities and requirements to restore their productive capacities.

(b) In some countries with economies dependent on an extractive industry, like oil production in Iraq and aluminum ore mining in Guinea, restoring the production operations will be a high priority. Restoration of revenue-earning enterprises can contribute to accelerating recovery.

(c) Private sector enterprises are generally left to their own means to restore their activities. State-owned enterprises, on the other hand, are usually problematic. If they have not been profitable, and if the new government plans to introduce policy reforms to develop a free market economy, closing them might be the appropriate decision. But as in Iraq, if these enterprises employ significant numbers of people, with unemployment a serious problem, putting more people out of work and increasing the availability of people subject to recruitment by terrorist groups is undesirable. An assessment of restoration of public sector enterprises has to be done in conjunction with the economic assessments. Chapter III continues this discussion.

(10) **Public Buildings and Cultural Facilities**. HN authorities frequently request that cultural facilities; such as temples, museums, monuments, and cemeteries be assessed for reconstruction requirements. These requests can be accommodated, but rarely carry much priority for funding. For steady-state Phase 0 operations, supporting these facilities is rarely considered. It would take very special circumstances for cultural facilities to be considered for a project.

6. Establish a Time Horizon

a. **General**. An important first step will be aligning military plans with the three time horizons considered standard within the larger development community:

(1) Short Term: 3-18 months;

(2) Mid-Term: 18 months to 3-4 years;

(3) Long Term: 3-4 years to 10+ years.

b. Post-conflict stabilization and reconstruction planning and implementation are conducted in conditions sharply different from those of normal infrastructure construction projects. Political time lines prevail. The desire to achieve larger stabilization and reconstruction objectives to conform with political objectives will bring pressures to bear on the planning process (e.g., oil production and power generation in Iraq to meet production targets, and building the ring road in Afghanistan). The pressures are bi-directional. Efforts to accommodate the political time-lines are appropriate. At the same time, planners and managers must also clearly and sometimes assertively communicate the risks and limitations involved in adjusting reconstruction schedules to meet political objectives. Therefore, setting overly optimistic schedules for infrastructure construction can be counter-productive.

c. The major political time-lines are the dates set for turning over authority for operations to other entities. The interagency strategic plan approved by the CRSG sets interim objectives that are often guided by political milestones (e.g., dates for placing host government officials in positions of authority, elections, and establishing new HN institutions). It is important for planners to participate in the development and adjustment over time of the strategic plan to assure that the time-lines of infrastructure construction are realistic.

d. Past experience indicates that post-conflict ES&CI restoration likely will last for years. It is important to recognize that the planning and operational requirements vary for the different periods of the post-conflict efforts. Also, steady-state Phase 0 planning has very different time requirements. The possibilities are outlined below.

e. **Intervention Phases**. Design and planning requirements are different in different phases of an intervention, in large measure defined by the presence, or lack thereof, of an active US embassy or consular presence in the country and the absorptive capacity of the national government. This translates directly into the quality and availability of current in-country information. The initial intervention period, up to three months, will likely require a complete revision of the pre-deployment plan based on information now available. The transition period, lasting for the next several months up to two years, can be sufficient to complete the intervention objectives in some situations. US experiences in Bosnia, Haiti, East Timor, Kosovo, Afghanistan, and Iraq demonstrate that significant deficiencies in the political, societal, and economic situations will require long-term recovery efforts, which can take a decade or more.

(1) **Pre-deployment Phase**. In general, joint operation design and planning with the participation of the AMEMB staff will incorporate more accurate in-country information. Also in general, for countries with an AMEMB, the chances are that an "intervention" will be less complex. The most important design and planning activities for ES&CI restoration will be to gather information on existing public services, both performance statistical data, to serve as a baseline for determining metrics requirements, and the physical location of facilities.

(2) **Early Intervention Phase**. The most critical planning takes place during the first few weeks of an intervention. This is the time when a new and unknown power structure (i.e., the intervention force) will be creating a new environment where new institutional practices can be most easily established. It is the "Golden Hour" for intervening authorities, where they will enjoy the greatest credibility and tolerance from a host population anxious for their success. Since the crisis leading to the intervention is generally rife with governance deficiencies, improved systems will need to be put in place as soon as is practicable to correct them. Because of the dependency of HN authorities and populations on its proper functioning, ES&CI restoration likely provides the best opportunity to reform past practices. Thus, early assessments, design, and planning,

plus work with HN officials, are the most critical in an intervention. It is the most challenging period. Short-term imperatives must be addressed; but simultaneously, design and planning for the long-term, eventual TOA must begin.

(3) **Transition Phase**. Once the major priorities are addressed during the initial intervention phase, serious transition planning begins toward the established TOA. One major challenge of this phase is to accommodate requirements within the resources available. Resources for reconstruction are always limited; setting priorities and sequences of activities that will last through a transition period, and for the long-term reconstruction effort beyond, based on resources that are expected to be available, is a primary concern. Some aspects of the Golden Hour last through this phase. For the infrastructure reconstruction effort, it is critical to establish the appropriate regulatory and management infrastructure for the HN governance process during this period. Essential services restoration to normal operation should occur during this phase.

(4) **Long-Term Reconstruction Phase**. All the requirements necessary to achieve an effective TOA will be the priority for this phase. Infrastructure reconstruction projects take long periods to complete. New regulatory and management structures also take a long time to create, test, refine, and institutionalize.

CHAPTER III
CROSS-SECTOR PLANNING CONSIDERATIONS

1. The Military Problem

> **How can a military commander set the conditions for effective long-term development of essential services and supporting infrastructure during the limited time of military engagement in a crisis region?**

a. There is strong consensus among the interagency community that balance is required between providing **physical infrastructure** - which graphically shows progress - and developing the **organizations, management skills, and institutions** that, while less glamorous, all provide incentives and structure for the long-term viability of the physical project. It is critical that political and military leaders in the US and in the HN understand that effective infrastructure development takes many years to reach fruition; and that near-term gains that cannot be sustained are of little long-term value, and generally entail significant opportunity costs. Keeping this perspective in focus is contrary to the organizational imperative to produce immediate measurable results during a relatively short tour, with no accountability for failures that occur due to systemic flaws after that tour has ended. As is the case with many challenges, the professionalism required to pursue maximum long-term benefits is often in direct conflict with the careerism that rewards the perception of near-term success. The pursuit of professionalism when it is in conflict with careerism will require decision makers of great character, as well as aptitude.

b. As was noted earlier in this handbook, the ultimate goal of a ES&CI intervention should be directed toward restoring, strengthening, and in some cases establishing for the first time, the capacity of the HN to effectively produce and manage critical services for its citizenry. Accordingly, joint operation plans should be informed by a set of principles congruent with the larger interagency community.

2. Expectation Management: Demonstrate Visible Progress

a. The JFC must be very careful to not communicate that things will quickly be getting better than they were before the intervention. Rather, key services indices will likely need to be designed, and as much as practicable, sequenced to support the concept of local control and responsibility for utility services. Although it may be difficult to accept, one of the most important initial messages that must be clearly understood by HN leaders, opinion-makers, and the general population is that recovery from a crisis, particularly in the case of major conflict, is not rapid or easily accomplished. Local expectations are invariably high for favorable change, and for donors to contribute substantial funds and foreign experts to repair damage in a very short time. In Iraq, the slow reconstruction efforts were criticized because of the expectations of the country that landed a man on the moon. This resulted in the United States being blamed for deliberately responding slowly for political reasons.

b. The "street lights first" concept (see vignette below) during Liberia's post-civil war period (2005-06) demonstrated several key messages in support of the Liberian government that were instrumental in sustaining the peace, namely:

(1) Local authorities can provide dependable power.

(2) Local authorities are concerned for nighttime security.

(3) Stable energy supplies will attract private sector investment, create viable jobs, and improve Liberia's economic condition.

STREET LIGHTS FIRST

USAID is supporting two big energy projects in Liberia. One is the Emergency Power Program (EPP) which is providing electricity supply, on a full cost recovery basis, including network rehabilitation and maintenance, for emergency power supply in Monrovia. The objective is to provide electricity, especially streetlights, to additional neighborhoods in Monrovia, affecting as many as 300,000 residents. The second program, the Liberian Energy Assistance Program, aims to increase access to affordable energy supplies in order to foster economic, political, and social development in Liberia. The primary methods of doing this will be pilots of sustainable energy service delivery in urban poor neighborhoods; renewable electricity pilots in rural areas; and support of the energy sector reform process to attract private sector investment. While the first project is focused on emergency power supply in order to promote political stability, the second is trying to lay the groundwork for long-term economic development.

A note on the streetlights: Achievements of the first phase of the EPP project include provision of electricity service to businesses and social institutions in two areas of Monrovia, which contain about 25% (190,000) of the city's population, and provision of 272 streetlights. The streetlights hold political significance; during her inaugural address on January 16, 2006, President Johnson-Sirleaf promised to bring electricity to Monrovia within her first 150 days in office. The successful commencement of electricity supply on July 26, 2006, Liberia's Independence Day, symbolized her commitment to the Liberian people. The emergency electricity provision was an important part of the political stabilization process, as well as a step toward an economically more sustainable provision of electricity service. Although it's a small step, it's in the right direction. The message is "small light today, big light tomorrow."

USAID (by permission)
http://www.travelpod.com/travel-blog-entries/sharbear427/liberia-2007jan/
1168728060/tpod.html

---

c. Similarly, as shown in the text box that follows, the restoration of streetcar service in Sarajevo provided visible evidence of the return to normalcy without creating undue expectations for major enhancements in transportation infrastructure.

SARAJEVO STREETCARS

Within days following NATO intervention in Sarajevo in 1994 the Bosnians had their highly used streetcars up and running, which was both symbolic of the peace brought by the cease-fire and provided necessary city transportation. The Bosnians had been remarkably ingenious during the period the Serbs surrounded Sarajevo. They brought in electrical lines from Bosnian power plants, and food supplies through a tunnel under the airport. As a result, reconstruction efforts in Bosnia proceeded relatively easily, as contrasted with the more difficult governance transformation process.

VARIOUS SOURCES

d. When considering the range of necessary infrastructure projects, joint force planners must be highly attuned to the message an infrastructure project and supported services will project to the local population, and to others. Messages can range from, "We are here to provide the most rudimentary assistance to prevent the loss of life" to "We are here to create from the wreckage of your city a world-class utility grid," and every shade of gray in between. **Under virtually all circumstances, the message should be: "We are here to assist your government."**

e. The decision on what projects to address, and how and when to address them, must also be attenuated by a highly developed sense of cultural sensitivity, including potentially limiting the scope and complexity of a project to conform to local conditions, as opposed to implementing full-blown Western considerations of what would be desirable. Pre-project consultations with HN central and local governments, as well as USAID's representatives at the embassy, should help scope a project concept to remain within the art of the possible. USAID's contacts with the local NGO community can also be an important planning resource.

3. Ownership Issues

a. Full Privatization

(1) A fundamental question that must be addressed at the beginning of the planning process will be public versus private ownership of the infrastructure project. USAID's broad experience in this area concludes that in most circumstances, private ownership is the desired end state. For joint planners therefore, the new regulatory environment under their purview should be structured accordingly.

(2) The shift to privatization in infrastructure and utility operation represents a profound reassessment of conventional public policy. The old and deceptively simple model of state ownership is rife with underinvestment, under-pricing (revenue inadequacy), high costs, low productivity, poor service quality, theft of service, political interference, and a general lack of transparency. USAID has found that privatization, if accompanied by unbundling of assets and regulatory reform, offers the highest potential for increased investment, cost-reflective tariffs, incentives for efficiency, access to superior management

and service quality, political insulation and greater transparency. All of these factors are crucial for long-term effectiveness of the utility or infrastructure project.

(3) Prerequisites for effective privatization include[22]:

(a) a suitable set of institutions, legal system, and a country-specific strategy;

(b) a market-friendly institutional framework;

(c) a macroeconomic structure open to competition; and

(d) an effective system of regulation; specifically designed around coherence, independence, accountability, predictability, and capacity.

(4) Key stakeholders in any privatization plan will include: shareholders, politicians, boards, regulators, business managers and, at the end of the chain, the customers who will both consume the service and pay the tariffs.

(5) Three "hard spots" in particular will attend any privatization initiative:

(a) **Pricing reform**; there must be a satisfactory balance between social equity and actual business needs.

(b) **Access to bottleneck facilities**, i.e., having some level of control or influence on the single points of failure such as telecommunications, electrical grid, railroad tracks, etc., without which other services will fail.

(c) **Regionalizing infrastructure policy**; creating a regulatory environment supporting mutual markets that transcend national boundaries.

b. **Partial Privatization**

"Most government-owned utilities in developing countries perform poorly when judged as providers of electricity, in part because politicians and officials use their power, not to encourage the utilities to increase sales, improve the collection of bills, and cut costs, but to transfer resources to politically influential groups and, sometimes, extract bribes. To improve the performance of government-owned electricity utilities as electricity utilities, rules and practices must be changed in a way that reduces politicians' willingness or ability to use the utilities for political purposes and subjects the utilities to new sources of pressure to perform well... [G]overnments should be cautious about the prospects for improvement without privatization since, among other things, creating a truly arms-length relationship between the government and the utility will always be difficult as long as the government remains the utility's owner- but [] improvements in corporate governance are still worth pursuing."[24]

(1) In some circumstances, the joint force may find that local political leaders or the prevailing political culture may be "unwilling to risk the certain controversy and possible loss of support that privatization may entail..."[23] In this case, joint force infrastructure planners must look at the option of improving, as far as possible, the performance of a state-owned utility, particularly as it relates to the relationship between the business itself and its government "owners." The underlying issue will be improving, and in some cases developing from scratch, a climate of highly professional corporate governance.

(2) Assuming there are credible local authorities with whom to consult and/or negotiate, it will be critical for the HN government to make a viable commitment to cost-covering tariffs (or a cost-covering combination of tariffs and subsidies). Without such a commitment, private investors will most likely not buy into the utility. Strong consideration must also be given to reducing the government's fundamental conflict of interest in being both the owner and manager of the utility. The below listed objectives should help mitigate the problem of government-owned utilities:

(a) Reducing the net benefit to politicians and officials who use utilities to achieve political goals in non-transparent ways; this can be done by either raising the cost or reducing the benefit.

(b) Subjecting the utilities to commercial pressures from sources other than the government (i.e., commercial financing standards of performance).

(c) Removing or alleviating the conflict of interest the government faces as owner and policy maker.

4. Cost Recovery

a. **General**. In the realm of intervention-related infrastructure development, particularly regarding utilities, planners must keep in mind the long-term nature of the project, which by necessity means that the local population must, in one way or another, act as true customers, and actually pay for the services they receive from the utility. As part of the larger reform of a utility, cost recovery is often less an issue of willingness to pay and more an issue of willingness to charge.

b. Operating costs will include, among others, salaries, energy, costs of goods or services sold, maintenance, information technology, capital costs including debt and equity, etc. Long term success for a complex project demands contract agreements and operating plans designed from the start to create a system that is financially solvent. THERE IS NO FREE LUNCH. Planners must work with local authorities and civic leaders to help develop a "culture of payment" with the recipient population.

c. Project costs may be direct, as noted above, or hidden. Security concerns in particular have been shown to add up to 20% of an enterprise's operating expenses. In this regard, military planners may not even be aware of the extent to which their normal force protection posture would add to a utility's budget once the intervention force is re-deployed, assuming concomitant security requirements remain steady. Turnover plans should factor this into the equation.

d. **Getting Services to the Poor**. A key subset of cost recovery will be designing a system that will help ensure continued delivery of utility services to the poor. Direct subsidies should be avoided, where possible, as they will generally create a situation where customers and managers will lose the will to work toward actual cost recovery. A subsidized "safety net" of sorts can be designed, but can only be effective if the households are legally connected to the system and accurately metered. Poorly designed subsidies will often have the unintended consequence of encouraging inefficient consumption by the household and provide disincentives for the utility to reduce costs and/or expand their service. Given the above, several subsidy concepts can be explored:

(1) **Consumption-based** — the simplest to administer, but generally the least effective, establishing progressive rates for higher levels of consumption.

(2) **Geographical Targeting** — setting a standardized rate for particular areas, like segregated slums.

(3) **Means Testing** — requires a high administrative capacity in the utility, but provides a good level of return against the subsidy.

(4) **Self-Selection of Service Levels** — applying varying tariffs against variable service levels allows for more accurate pricing while supporting a baseline service level.

(5) **Connection Subsidies** — applying the subsidy to the cost of connecting a household into the formal system, but charging a nominal standardized tariff for core utility services.

e. Other considerations for getting services to the poor may include:

(1) increasing flexibility in payments to match households' income flow;

(2) higher billing frequency (i.e., lower individual bills);

(3) pre-payment systems;

(4) conservation: use of consumption-limiting devices;

(5) flexible standards (i.e., not applying US/European Union standards of service across the board); and

(6) easing legal restrictions to allow for alternative service providers (i.e., not forcing use of a municipal utility, allowing independent vendors to do business).

f. **Bottom Line**: There is no easy way around the need to increase levels of cost recovery if services are to be improved and expanded.

5. Contracting as a Management Tool

a. Planners will need to distinguish between contracting for construction services and creating operating contracts to manage re-established utility services. This section will focus on operating contracts as a tool in the utility's corporate governance framework.

b. In many post-conflict and natural disaster scenarios, simply rebuilding the infrastructure and turning it back to local authorities will not ensure improved services. USAID has learned over the years that the use of **incentive-based operating contracts** will often mitigate the original weak capacity of the utility staff. Several important features are common across the varying types of incentive contracts as follows:

(1) The contract is designed to put an operator in place to run the full scope of the utility business; including production, transmission, distribution, and commercial functions.

(2) The contract need not follow a single template (i.e., management contract, lease, or concession).

(3) The contract is "incentive-based" in that, to a notable extent, the operator's compensation is linked directly to performance of the enterprise. Poor performance would yield only a base fee that may not cover all costs. On the other hand, if they perform extremely well, they can earn a substantial performance-linked bonus. Three types of operating contracts are generally used during development projects:

(a) **Management Contract** — outlines management responsibility with limited operational and commercial control, and no private investment.

(b) **Concession** — grants full management and commercial control, with the operator making all investments and, by extension, the profits.

(c) **Affermage (Lease)** — widely used in Europe since the mid-19th century. Awards of leases are made by competitive tender or negotiation to a private firm to run a system for a period of years. Lessee is responsible for operational and commercial functions, and receives a fixed fee per unit of water or electricity provided to customers. Government provides the fixed capital investment.

GENERAL GUIDELINES WHEN CONSIDERING EMPLOYMENT OF INCENTIVE-BASED CONTRACTING AS A MANAGEMENT TOOL[25]

a. Well-designed operating contracts can lead to reduced technical and commercial losses, increased billing and collection rates and introduction of efficient and accountable management.

b. Contract design must fit the local situation: successful models include advisory contracts, management contracts, divesture with regulation, incentive-based management with former employees, and lease and concession

---

contracts. The majority of contracts used some form of strong incentive to force the operator to rapidly improve performance, followed by targets for realistic long-term performance. Contract terms may start out as short as two years, with 7-10 years becoming the norm for lease contracts where operators are expected to invest their own capital in some aspect of the business.

c. Publicly-owned corporations can also work well with strong incentive mechanisms.

d. Contracts should deal with critical design issues, including:

(1) covering accumulated losses during a transitional period;

(2) providing reasonably high levels of operator autonomy and operational control;

(3) striving for competitive bidding but allowing for single negotiations as an alternative; and

(4) linking incentives directly to performance and making them large enough to drive behavior. Several types of incentives are available:

(a) progressive annual performance targets;

(b) multi-year or end of contract performance targets;

(c) operating margins where the operator seeks to maximize earnings by reducing losses and costs; and

(d) fixed price per unit delivered, billed and collected.

e. Risk allocation should be clear and fair.

f. Operator should have full control over the business, assets, and staff.

g. Collection of reliable data (i.e. metering) is critical to shifting risk to a private operator.

h. Low capital investment may be preferable to huge investments at the start of a contract. Initial emphasis would concentrate on institutional, management and personnel reforms, emergency rehabilitation, and rebuilding relationships with customers.

i. Practical dispute resolution mechanisms and financial models can forestall contract failure. This is particularly important to help manage the relationship between the stakeholders, the asset holding company and government ministries.

j. If the starting condition of a utility is bad, start with short contracts that emphasize:

(1) enumeration of customers;

(2) regularization of illegal customers;

(3) inventory and assessment of physical assets;

(4) set up new commercial and financial systems, with emphasis on new billing and collection capabilities;

(5) introduce new personnel systems to ID employees, create effective supervisory relationships and weed out corrupt staff;

(6) introduce bulk and consumer metering;

(7) establish reliable supply schedules with gradual increases in supply; and

(8) complete an emergency rehabilitation program.

k. Tariff increases should be gradual and should match improvements in services.

l. Expect wide variation in the cost of tendering and developing operating contracts.

m. An effective regulatory framework can enhance success, but is not crucial if well-designed regulation can be written directly into a contract.

6. Business, Legal and Regulatory Environment

"Your normal World Bank client just wants to build stuff. But if you had a 'normal' business, you would certainly do the groundwork before you start. You need to consider what you do as a business, not a social service."

World Bank Development Officer
December 2007

a. Infrastructure is not just physical facilities. It is often a set of businesses that own, operate, and renew infrastructure facilities. A joint force is likely to be required to reform an existing enabling environment under which the infrastructure operates. This will involve "fixing" corporate form and governance, laws, regulation, public funding, capital markets, infrastructure institutions, and facilities. It is the business that operates and maintains the system. As such, a "bankable" utility:

(1) has enough cash to pay all its costs, including operational and capital costs;

(2) has a predictable means of recovering its revenue requirements;

(3) has sufficient financial controls to meet high standards of creditworthiness; and

(4) can deal with the financial risks that happen in the normal course of business.

b. It is important that statutory authorities for government operation exist before expectation of government performance can be realized. The Civil Aviation Authority, for example, cannot manage safety unless it has authority, in law, to conduct surveillance, impose penalties, etc. Although legislative affairs are beyond the scope of this handbook, ES&CI practitioners will be highly affected by the larger environment of a fragile or recovering government structure.

c. The joint force may be intervening in a societal environment where some level of regulation was already in place, but is now at some other level dysfunctional. In that case, reforms to existing structures must "begin at the beginning," fixing the corporate form and governance, getting the sector structure and enabling environment right, with the recognition that costs will ratchet up as the full nature of the service-infrastructure system builds to maturity. Sequencing the reconstruction is vitally important and runs from the cheap (e.g., enacting law, establishing regulation and private sector participation [PSP]) to the mixed costs of credit enhancements, improved bureaucratic efficiency, and access for the poor to the expensive (e.g., physical utility construction, distribution systems, renewable energy).

d. Key indicators of an effective business environment include:

(1) improved mechanisms for enforcing contracts;

(2) improving employment law;

(3) simplifying tax administration; and

(4) improved political governance (i.e., improved accountability of the government to its citizens).

e. Planners who are facing the task of establishing a reformed regulatory environment should begin with a thorough review of the Organization for Economics Cooperation and Development (OECD) *Principles of Corporate Governance (2004)*, which is summarized in the box below. The OECD principles focus on governance problems that result from the separation of ownership and control. Corporate governance involves a set of relationships between a company's management, its board, its shareholders, and other stakeholders. Corporate governance also provides the structure through which the objectives of the company are set, and the means of attaining those objectives and monitoring performance are determined. Good corporate governance should provide proper incentives for the board and management to pursue objectives that are in the interests of the company and its shareholders, and should facilitate effective monitoring. The principles are summarized below:

f. Bottom Line for Military Planners

OECD PRINCIPLES OF CORPORATE GOVERNANCE

I. The corporate governance framework should promote transparent and efficient markets, be consistent with the rule of law, and clearly articulate the division of responsibilities among different supervisory, regulatory, and enforcement authorities.

II. The corporate governance framework should protect and facilitate the exercise of shareholders' rights.

III. The corporate governance framework should ensure the equitable treatment of all shareholders, including minority and foreign shareholders. All shareholders should have the opportunity to obtain effective redress for violation of their rights.

IV. The corporate governance framework should recognize the rights of stakeholders established by law or through mutual agreements and encourage active cooperation between corporations and stakeholders in creating wealth, jobs, and the sustainability of financially sound enterprises.

V. The corporate governance framework should ensure that timely and accurate disclosure is made on all material matters regarding the corporation; including the financial situation, performance, ownership, and governance of the company.

VI. The corporate governance framework should ensure the strategic guidance of the company, the effective monitoring of management by the board, and the board's accountability to the company and the shareholders.

---

(1) Design and plan through regulatory and governance structures before taking physical actions.

(2) Consult with local leadership and higher level political players.

(3) Consult with USG civilian agencies, especially USAID-EGAT in coordination with the US embassy.

(4) Study the full OECD Corporate Governance document which can be found online at http://www.oecd.org/dataoecd/32/18/31557724.pdf.

7. Maintenance Standards

a. From the moment a project or piece of equipment comes into being, it begins an inexorable process of deterioration. This is called "entropy," and it affects all things (maturity naturally being followed by decay in biological and organizational entities). During a crisis intervention, normal long-term maintenance requirements for facilities and equipment are often rightly put aside in favor of more immediate operational results.

Additionally, the majority of military interventions likely will be into areas and cultures where Western standards of maintenance are only honored by exception. Therefore, for joint force efforts to have a lasting effect, the programs and systems must be designed with the expectation of inadequate maintenance.

    b. Maintenance mitigation can be resolved in part by:

        (1) simplicity of design;

        (2) carefully designed exterior structures addressing drainage, ultraviolet exposure, temperature fluctuations, wind, dust intrusion, environmental hazards, etc;

        (3) minimized reliance on external servicing;

        (4) minimized exposure to "bottleneck facilities" that provide single-point failure downstream from the subject facility;

        (5) use of equipment selected for high reliability;

        (6) use of designs that are over-built and under-operated; and

        (7) acceptance of functional capabilities that may not meet normal Western standards, but which are acceptable to local populations.

    c. Project managers can accomplish multiple goals by enlisting local populations for ongoing maintenance efforts. In addition to keeping projects functioning, employing locals can create over the long-term a small business or team of businesses that supports broader economic growth in the community. A good example of this may be found in an ongoing Peruvian road maintenance project undertaken by the Word Bank and Inter-American Development Bank (see vignette below). In this situation, the government of Peru desired to initiate a project to help alleviate chronic poverty in its mountainous rural areas. The result was an innovative rural roads maintenance project.

RURAL ROAD MAINTENANCE IN PERU

    In response to the government of Peru's desire to alleviate chronic poverty in its rural areas, World Bank and the Inter-American Development Bank in 1996 instituted a rural roads maintenance and poverty alleviation project whose goal was to integrate poorly accessible areas to markets and other economic drivers, to generate employment and stimulate further income-earning activities in rural areas, and to strengthen local institutional activities to manage rural road networks. The project continues to this writing (2009). Specific emphasis is on rehabilitation of the rural area's "networking" capability- the gravel roads and non-motorized paths, followed by 670 maintenance contracts performed by community-based micro-enterprises.

    Project managers held extensive consultations and preparatory workshops to: a) assess real transportation needs, b) understand poverty links as perceived

---

by the community, c) confirm priority of works and the community's commitment to its maintenance, d) validate designs and include local solutions, e) mobilize local government support for road building and institution building, and finally, f) build up ownership with key stakeholders concerning strategies and proposed actions.

By including local participation early on, the World Bank and Inter-American Development Bank planners gained a fuller understanding of transportation needs as perceived by the communities, and gained important 'buy-in' by women's groups and local governments as the full scope of the project became a shared objective.

A key portion of the project was the creation and financing of contractual relationships with over 670 micro-enterprises, who maintain over 15,000 km of roads and 3000 km of trails. The project emphasizes that this is not welfare; the results of micro-enterprises contracting provided a cost-effective solution to the problem of year-round accessibility on gravel roads. It created a catalyst for local development by providing entrepreneurial capacity in the community, bringing in new services and stimulating labor markets. The project stimulated the development of 38 provincial road institutes responsible for road maintenance within their jurisdiction.

The project used a number of innovative metrics to measure effectiveness; specific survey criteria are noted in Appendix C, "Sample Metrics."

VARIOUS SOURCES

8. Security Issues

a. Construction of security boundaries and other protection infrastructure is a well-understood military mission that will not be addressed in this handbook other than to point out that if physical security for facilities and local populations is not assured first, very little else can be constructively accomplished. In the absence of physical security, workers can be driven away, facilities destroyed, and local populations terrorized into submission to, or even cooperation with, adversaries. That said, civilian-oriented ES&CI restoration efforts demand attention to the latent security situation, particularly when undertaken in a non-permissive (i.e., uncertain) operational environment.

b. **Special Security Considerations for Civilian Infrastructure**. It is impossibly costly to erect enough dedicated security infrastructure to protect all essential services facilities. As a result, cost effectiveness calculations are required. For facilities with high-value assets (e.g., power plants, water pumping facilities), it is cost-effective to protect those assets with physical security infrastructure. However, for facilities that have extensive distribution systems (e.g., power transmission lines, underground water pipes) where physical security infrastructure becomes far more expensive than simply replacing damaged property, it will not be cost-effective. The greatest security in many cases is provided by sympathetic local populations. If they can be kept secure against external threats, they can multiply the effectiveness of physical security precautions and discourage adversary actions.

NOTE: *At times it can be cost effective to construct parallel, redundant, or "looped" systems to thwart the effect of damage (e.g., road systems or electrical transmission lines that connect at geographic intervals and/or at the extremities so traffic or electricity can flow back around the damaged loops).*

INFRASTRUCTURE SECURITY IN SARAJEVO

Essential services facilities (e.g., water sources, purification and distribution systems, market areas, electrical production and distribution systems, and municipal central heating systems) are often priority targets with political significance on both sides of a conflict equation. For example, the Serbs controlled the water and natural gas input to Sarajevo city and frequently turned them off to suit their interests. Even so, international response to Bosnia stagnated for two years (1992-4) until a market was mortared in early 1994, killing dozens. The attack was covered by major news media (the National Broadcasting Company anchor news reporter happened to be in Sarajevo at the time) and this "last straw" atrocity caused NATO to take action and force Serb guns from around the city, eventually resulting in a coercive intervention in 1995 by Implementation Force.

---

c. **Shared or Adjacent Civilian and Military Facilities**

(1) Some facilities serve both civilian and military functions. Airports, seaports, and some government buildings (e.g., Ministries of Defense) are examples. This obligates military planners to work with civilian counterparts in the design and management of infrastructure construction. Infrastructure designed for force protection may need to be extended to the protection of associated civilian facilities.

SHARED USE OF CIVILIAN AND MILITARY FACILITIES

Sharing headquarters facilities during initial intervention operations can also become contentious without adequate considerations for both civilian and military needs. The Task Force Alpha military commander for Operation PROVIDE COMFORT in Northern Iraq in 1991 established his headquarters in an abandoned grain processing facility. This facility was also the headquarters for the civilian HA team (this was truly a joint civil-military operation), and was critical as a center for the food relief program for the civilians. But security procedures for the military also inhibited free access by NGOs to the civilian team and inconvenienced the use of the grain storage and processing facilities.

---

(2) This obligation requires extending the assessment of requirements for shared facilities to use based on rapidly increasing civil-military emergency requirements during the early days of an intervention, as well as projected joint use requirements

throughout the crisis response period. One good example is the joint use of very congested airfield facilities in Albania during the early Kosovo intervention period. While security wasn't a major concern for this facility, it is one of the better examples of competing priorities and how rapidly infrastructure requirements can arise in crisis responses.

d. Promoting a "Permissive" Environment for Civilian Engagement

(1) Civilian deployment for crisis response operations requires establishing security conditions for them to operate with limited risk. Civilians have used the term "permissive" for the conditions under which they will deploy. "Permissive" has been defined differently over time, so the first task is to determine, for any given operation, how it is defined for that instance (such determinations may change over time). During the last decade, "permissive" meant a complete cessation of hostilities. The conditions in Afghanistan and Iraq required a significant change in that definition. Although civilians are increasingly willing to risk their lives to accomplish national security objectives, all necessary provisions to assure civilian security and minimize the risk to civilians remain necessary.

(2) The office of first responsibility for determining security risks to USG civilian and other US citizens is State Department's Office of Diplomatic Security (State/DS). That office is represented in the field by the RSO at the AMEMB.

(3) When the JFC places a high priority on establishing conditions for civilians to deploy, it will likely require providing civilians the same protection for their facilities as the military provides for itself. But planning for constructing protection infrastructure needs to be done according to specifications provided by the civilians themselves, usually from State/DS and USAID security officials. The facilities that require protection include facilities where the civilians work with their HN counterparts, such as the ministry offices and work spaces near construction sites.

(4) Protection of civilians may occasionally extend to coalition partners, and HN officials and populations when deemed a priority; although this responsibility generally exceeds military mandates and resources. The famous "Green Zone" in Baghdad is the clearest example of this being done, where Iraqi government officials were housed and worked from the protected zone. Establishing protection zones could also secure zones for IDP and refugee camps, particularly if preventing human rights violations is at stake.

e. Environmental Factors. Planners expecting a permissive environment may instead find troops in a suddenly non-permissive (i.e., uncertain or hostile) one or vice versa. As the Haitian case illustrates in the below vignette, uncertainty required planners to prepare multiple options for many contingencies; while the East Asian Tsunami case illustrates prudent planning can help turn a potentially dangerous environment into a peaceful one. Capability packages, therefore, should be sufficiently diversified and flexible to allow deployed forces to accomplish their missions at varying levels of permissiveness.

PERMISSIVENESS

Chief among environmental factors affecting needed US capabilities for stability operations is permissiveness. Permissiveness is determined by the level of hostility that US personnel encounter during entry or at any other time during an operation.

Stability operations in Afghanistan, the Horn of Africa, and Kosovo were all conducted in semi-permissive environments, both at the time of entry and throughout the operation. In the case of Operation UPHOLD DEMOCRACY in Haiti, US and multinational forces entered into a permissive environment and expected it to persist. Yet enemy resistance never materialized, and the United States conducted the remainder of its mission in a permissive environment.

The East Asian Tsunami relief effort constituted the only true case of permissiveness among the five stability operations cited. To be sure, the operation occurred in a region previously home to considerable hostility, and there were isolated threats to US troops. But US planners mitigated these potential risks and enhanced force protection by establishing a very small land footprint and sea basing the vast majority of soldiers. As a consequence, the United States preserved the permissive environment.

The insights gleaned from these experiences clearly illustrate that permissiveness is a dynamic—not static—variable in stability operations.

To prepare, DOD had produced two plans, one for an operation with "offensive violence inflicted suddenly, from air and sea, with overwhelming but appropriate force" and another for peaceful entry.

James Dobbins et.al.,
America's Role in Nation-Building: From Germany to Iraq,
(Santa Monica, CA: RAND, 2003), p. 137.[26]

f. **Police Facilities**

(1) During recent deployments where re-establishing security conditions have been a severe challenge, the role of the HN police has been both critical and problematic. They generally are not equipped to protect themselves adequately against today's terrorists and insurgents. Mission success often depends on how well the HN's police forces can be trained and equipped to perform their jobs effectively and responsibly. Construction of police facilities is likely to be part of a post-conflict reconstruction requirement, possibly constructed to specifications normally used for military facilities.

(2) The biggest challenge may be to assist the police in establishing facilities that permit them to be more effective at fulfilling their "community policing" responsibilities. In democratic governments, police are responsible to the communities in which they work, a change from being subordinate to authoritarian governments. This requires that police have facilities to meet with community groups and leaders, often separate from

their police facilities, to work toward improving their policing functions. If security conditions are acceptable, and if these meeting facilities exist, they should be of high priority for providing security infrastructure.

CONSIDERATIONS WHEN BUILDING POLICE FACILITIES

"The majority of police station construction in Iraq has been performed by contract ... This model can be and has been successful, but requiring the contractor to provide enough security to defend against sustained, complex attacks without assistance is cost-prohibitive ... Without committed forces there is minimal chance for successfully completing any construction. This ... makes a construction site, otherwise insignificant to ground combat element commanders, a friendly operational objective for their combat forces. [This] may not feel like a natural choice for combat commanders ... [but] if full consideration is given to the level of effect [from] an operating police force, the decision becomes much easier.

"The question of where and when to build police stations can create a 'chicken and egg' scenario. Should stations be built to consolidate gains where the conditions are safe enough to build without expectation of incidents, or should stations be built where conditions are poor so the police can help shape conditions? ... On one hand, waiting for conditions to be safe enough to expect no incidents would create a timetable too long to be acceptable to commanders and not in concert with the theater strategy. On the other hand, charging into completely untamed areas (as may happen in Afghanistan) with only a construction crew would be asking for more setbacks than progress."[27]

---

9. Resourcing

a. **General**. The military and civilians follow starkly different planning processes with respect to resource availability. In general terms, military planning is conducted with a careful eye toward existing force structure (requirements vs. availability, readiness, operating tempo, etc.). However, beyond force apportionment, the military planner is essentially unconstrained. By comparison, civilian agencies always plan on the basis of the level of resources they are given or can expect to receive. For civilians, adjusting the level of resources available is an onerous process. The planning processes for stability operations are evolving for both. For the military, resource constraints are definitely becoming a part of its planning process. For civilians, the significantly increased requirements due to the importance of crisis response operations to US national security have resulted in sizeable increases in resources made available for these operations.

b. **Past resourcing models** include the following:

(1) **Military totally responsible** (e.g., post-World War II Germany and Japan). As a point of reference, the Marshall Plan wasn't begun immediately. It provided funding to new European governments who took the principal responsibility to manage their reconstruction.

(2) **Civilians totally responsible**; this was principally the case prior to 9/11.

(3) **Military** given the responsibility **in coordination with civilians** (e.g., Afghanistan and Iraq).

c. To facilitate unified action, a common set of assumptions must be co-developed, or at least coordinated, with relevant civilian agencies and other stakeholders, as appropriate. The core assumption for this handbook is that it will be an exceptional requirement for the military to be totally in charge and that follow-on civilian agencies will be deployed as early as possible. Military planners are obliged therefore to include planning for the transfer of their work to civilian agencies at some point. The accompanying assumption is that funding will be provided to civilian agencies in the traditional manner for the bulk of post-conflict ES&CI restoration management. Therefore the military, even if totally responsible at the outset, must from that outset plan with civilians to facilitate the eventual TOA. Accordingly, the manner in which funding will be provided at the outset of the post-conflict period to both military and civilian agencies will set the stage for determining how operations are planned and carried out.

d. If the JFC assumes that the joint force will be given initial responsibility for initiating all post-conflict ES&CI restoration activities, planners should arrange for funding needs to be brokered between and among all expected participating departments, with an eye to creating viable interagency agreements that will cover both the funding and the eventual TOA (discussed later in this chapter). The process of transferring funds in either direction will be complicated, and will involve early and detailed financial planning alongside operational planning.

e. **Resourcing ES&CI for Mission Accomplishment**

f. Today's irregular warfare requirements create conditions for simultaneous conflict and post-conflict planning. The supplemental budget appropriations for military purposes that are principally developed by the military alone can, and likely should, include post-conflict resources for initial and immediate repair of critical infrastructure; including repairs of infrastructure intentionally damaged or destroyed to achieve military purposes.

g. Examples of ES&CI restoration activities which are given high importance are the following:

(1) water pumping, purification, and distribution facilities;

(2) agriculture facilities necessary to restore agriculture production (e.g., farm equipment, roads for access, irrigation systems, and storage facilities);

(3) extending services to critical population groups (e.g., Sadr City in Baghdad);

(4) markets; and

(5) schools.

h. It is critical to estimate, as quickly as possible, the level of resources needed to perform the reconstruction required, and inform the interagency planning team, as well as the consequences of not performing the construction. This includes the variety of risks accompanying the projects, such as access or security constraints, that might hinder activities. Reasonable estimates can be provided in the pre-deployment period and updated when on the ground. The level of resources actually allocated for ES&CI projects will be determined by the planners as they calculate the priorities among competing major mission elements. Despite best efforts, planners must expect that resources will seldom be available at the level requested.

NOTE: *The discussion above is directed at the pre deployment and the first, immediate phase of interventions, when the intervening forces are required to address urgent requirements while the bulk of supplemental budgets are being developed. After intervention, HN authorities are themselves recovering from the crisis, organizing or reorganizing themselves, and have very limited capacities as a result. During this phase, it is at least difficult, if not counterintuitive, both to engage HN authorities in the planning and managing of reconstruction and to build resources into the budget for HN capacity building. But this is the beginning of the "Golden Hour." It is imperative to do whatever is possible to initiate the engagement of HN institutions and authorities in the design, planning, and operation of ES&CI restoration efforts, and to determine their capacities and potential resources (staff, management capabilities, budgets if they exist, equipment available, etc.). Assessment of HN resources forms the basis for determining the external resources required for the assistance programs.*

i. **Funding Allocation Through Operational Phases**

(1) Early operations generally will be funded by a budget supplemental. Depending on the scope of the operation, a subsequent supplemental may add additional funding, but these are considered undesirable. If further funding is required, Congress and Office of Management and Budget (OMB) expect USG agencies to include the funding requirements for post-conflict reconstruction programs in their normal operating year budgets (OYB). This poses three challenges for military planners. First, the design of the supplemental(s) needs to include launching long-term HN institution-building programs simultaneously while addressing immediate needs. Second, the military has not traditionally used its OYB to fund post-conflict reconstruction projects; in some circumstances, it can be proposed, specifically when dual-purpose civil-military projects are desirable (e.g., seaports, airports, and government security structures). Third, the expanded use of Commander's Emergency Response Program (CERP) funds from Afghanistan and Iraq to global use, with some of these funds used for infrastructure. This will tend to prolong the military's engagement in ES&CI restoration efforts during lengthy deployments.

(2) The military will not have the principal responsibility for planning and implementing the majority of long-term infrastructure efforts; but in those situations when it finds itself the sole authority on the ground, it has the responsibility to provide ES&CI assessment information to those who plan the long-term programs from the outset. For this reason, the JFC should solicit representatives of civilian agencies to embed early with deploying units to guide assessment and design efforts and to contribute to

developing the interagency "Strategic Plan," and its accompanying budget. Considerable tension usually exists between establishing funding priorities for addressing the immediate needs vs. assigning a priority for the long-term capacity-building. Mission success depends on the HN developing its capacity to manage ES&CI programs. Therefore, the faster this capacity is built, the earlier redeployment is possible.

(3) To address this, DOD is launching the "Building Partnership Capacity" program, whose funding begins in 2010. The content and criteria for this program are still being developed, and will likely evolve over time. But this new portfolio within DOD establishes an OYB budgetary line item that may be available to fund post-conflict capacity-building activities. As we assist HNs to build their own whole-of-government crisis management capacities, the military will be a significant partner in that newly developing endeavor, with funding possibly available to support the efforts.

(4) Some crisis responses can focus on limited geographic areas, such as the nation's capital; and crisis resolution is possible with a limited focus. Most recent experiences show that insurgencies can be widespread, forcing a gradual extension of stabilization efforts throughout the country. In these situations, the commander's CERP funds are especially valuable. These can be used for small-scale ES&CI projects appropriate for smaller cities and communities. They can extend over time throughout the intervention period; and because they are smaller, they have shorter individual time frames for completion. But the planning and design of these projects should also include examining local policies and institutions to assure that the legal and regulatory frameworks are in place. Capacity-building within a locality is as important as national capacity-building. In the end, the eventual TOA from the military to civilians, and to the HN government, depends on how well those capacity-building efforts are accomplished.

(5) The JFC will find that essential services activities will tend to decline rapidly once initially re-established; but the tension between simply restoring services vs. building greater capacity and technological upgrading will always exist. The latter is done as part of assisting in building a more effective and legitimate government which gains the respect of its populations. Justification for the use of relatively scarce resources to improve essential services facilities must therefore be presented on the basis of how it supports improved governance.

j. **Accountability, Auditing, and Financial Oversight**

SPECIAL INSPECTOR GENERAL FOR IRAQ RECONSTRUCTION REPORT

The significant amounts of funding disbursed to Iraq and Afghanistan have attracted the attention of Inspector General (IG) offices, OMB, Government Accounting Office, Congressional Research Service, and the media in general. All these offices deployed officers to the field to observe first hand how programs were managed. Congress established the Special Inspector General for Iraq Reconstruction (SIGIR) office to conduct program and financial audits of USG work in Iraq, and its mandate was extended to Afghanistan (www.sigir.mil/). SIGIR has conducted in-depth studies, deploying several auditors to Iraq. Its reports have been thorough and have indicated many weaknesses (http://www.sigir.mil/hardlessons/Default.aspx).

---

(1) Infrastructure reconstruction work brings with it significant amounts of resources to implement major works. However, without the proper legal authorities and regulatory institutions in place, it also brings the propensity for inefficiencies, exploitation, sub-standard work, and the re-establishment of economic conditions not conducive to stability and improved governance. Attention must be paid therefore to assisting the HN build the appropriate policies and effective institutions to deter criminality and corruption right from the outset.

(2) **The overall lesson is that a conscious and deliberate effort is needed to design accounting systems into reconstruction operations, and assign them sufficient priority to assure that they are effectively employed**. It is advisable to consult with the IG office to get advice on how to do this without detracting from operations. USAID's OFDA occasionally encountered accountability issues during its decades of conducting HA operations. Its consultations with USAID's IG office has resulted in a standard operating procedure to report any suspected inconsistency or missing resources. Professional accounting organizations are less concerned with the occasional inconsistency than with systemic neglect or abuse of accounting practices. Initial counseling and following good advice goes far to prevent bad reports and weak credibility of the operations.

(3) Two areas are particularly challenging as a post-conflict reconstruction accounting system is being designed. First, it is desirable to use HN contractors when possible; but accounting practices of these companies are designed traditionally to hide financial transactions because of authoritarian governments' exploitations; so ideally it would be good to train them in new practices. Second, HN government accounting practices are, in general, antiquated and designed to support non-transparent practices of authoritarian governments. Clearly professional, transparent accounting practices are not likely to exist; and it is nearly impossible to provide training to establish effective systems with HN organizations prior to conducting operations. But the need must not be neglected. The need to establish these kind of new policies and practices with HN authorities when the opportunity exists is related to "golden hour" considerations.

(4) This issue has not been adequately addressed in previous intervention experiences. Nor is it being given central attention yet by the wider USG interagency community. Lacking that, the military will need to determine what it will do for the next crisis response. To the extent that time permits, the pre-deployment phase is the time to design the systematic accounting practices and training programs for both HN contractors and government offices providing oversight to reconstruction. Designing rule of law and regulatory initiatives with the interagency teams assigned the rule of law MME will permit initiating institutional practices to the extent feasible upon deployment.

10. Authoritarian Societies and Corruption

"The core idea of modernization theory is that economic and technological development bring [with them] a coherent set of social, cultural, and political changes. A large body of empirical evidence supports this idea. Economic development is, indeed, strongly linked to pervasive shifts in people's beliefs and motivations, and these shifts in turn change the role of religion, job motivations, human fertility rates, gender roles and sexual norms. And they also bring growing mass demands for democratic institutions and for more responsive behavior on the part of elites."[28]

a. One common characteristic of most past crisis interventions is they are usually provoked by abuses instigated by authoritarian governance systems. Authoritarian governments often abuse their authority with impunity. Their practices are entrenched and permeate the country. A typical illustration is a pre-war Sierra Leonian provincial governor saying "a cow grazes where he stands." After intervention in countries like these, it takes years of significant effort to change hierarchical command structures, non-participating management styles, opaque financial practices, and governance policies that support autocratic rule.

b. Populations in authoritarian societies generally recognize and understand the governance systems employed, but have little choice but to live with them. More than that, anyone given a position of prominence assumes the right to do likewise. This carries forward even into a post-conflict reconstruction period where free market, participative societies are being constructed. One Iraqi minister who had been replaced confided to an expatriate, "my one regret is that I wasn't able to put aside several more millions of dollars while I served."

c. However, it is important to set reasonable goals regarding the mitigation of corruption, instituting anti-corruption standards that the people and culture are prepared to accept, rather than enforcing western standards regardless of the contexts.

d. The task to build a new, successful governance system in light of the past experiences and societal practices of the population in a country emerging from crisis is huge. At the same time, the immediate post-conflict period- the "Golden Hour" referred to earlier- provides the opportunity to establish the institutions and practices that lead to effective governance. Post-conflict reconstruction generally accepts the thesis that "modernization" will foster that path:

A WORLD BANK REPORT PROVIDES THE FOLLOWING PROGNOSIS, ALONG WITH LIBERIAN AND EAST TIMOR MANIFESTATIONS

"Countries emerging from civil wars are often marked by a history of societal fragmentation, exclusion, and civic disempowerment that lie at the very root of the conflict. Citizen-state relations deteriorate when public institutions become increasingly unaccountable and politically manipulated. The situation worsens further when the state turns against citizens, human rights violations become wide-spread, rule of law breaks down, violence ensues, and the state loses territorial control and the ability to protect its citizens from violence.

"In Liberia, years of public mismanagement, endemic corruption, and state abuse led to a long period of violent conflict and generated a high level of public cynicism. The post-conflict government now has to overcome cynicism to gain public support for its administrative reform and state-building processes. Achieving this objective inter alia depends on the state's willingness and capacity to constructively engage in the public sphere, to be transparent about activities and challenges encountered, and to be inclusive and responsive to public views and opinions. Timor-Leste and the violent unrest of 2006 provide us with an unfortunate example of a country paying a heavy price for the government's failure to engage constructively with its citizens in the post-conflict period.

"The creation of transparent and accountable institutions is recognized as central to successful post-conflict recovery."[29]

11. Transfer of Authority

a. Prior to Afghanistan and Iraq, interventions were seen as relatively short-term. The objectives were to stop the fighting and/or establish the conditions for successful relief operations. Once the objectives were achieved, the effort was transferred to another entity and the US military could redeploy. Transfer was usually to the United Nations (UN) (e.g., United Nations Operation in Somalia (UNOSOM) for Somalia, the Office of the High Representative for Bosnia, United Nations Stabilization Mission in Haiti (MINUSTAH) for Haiti). This will likely continue to be the case for future interventions. The decision to make such a TOA, determine which entity will take charge, set a schedule, determine if the US military will participate after the TOA, allocate resources to be used up to and after the TOA, and develop plans to assure progress will continue to achieve the long-term objectives of the intervention all have a bearing on infrastructure reconstruction planning.

b. Guidance for today's military operations assumes global conditions will require a US military presence for long-term operations. Mission objectives for these operations will focus on planning for and supporting an effective TOA to HN authorities. The achievement of the physical objectives of infrastructure construction has a significant political value; but the larger political objectives to establish an effective governance make it equally important, if not more important, to also establish effective institutions to manage infrastructure construction and the maintenance following the construction. Given the long-term nature and broad objectives of post-conflict reconstruction, there is sufficient time to work collaboratively with HN authorities to plan the training, and attend to the regulatory and management support requirements that support an effective TOA to the HN itself.

c. For normal post-conflict reconstruction efforts, the military will be working collaboratively with civilian entities. This includes US civilian agencies, other bilateral donor organizations (UK, France, Germany, and Japan aid agencies), and international organizations (World Bank, United Nations Development Program [UNDP]). It is a common objective for all to support a TOA to HN authorities. It is highly likely that when other agencies are able to be fully engaged in reconstruction activities, and their mandates include supporting long-term reconstruction and development assistance efforts, the US military will be able to do a TOA to those organizations for the activities the military has been performing. This simplifies the TOA requirement and should be considered an early planning goal.

Intentionally Blank

CHAPTER IV
METRICS—MEASURING PROGRESS

"You cannot manage what you do not measure."

Anonymous

1. The Competitive Requirements

The Military Problem: How can the commander create measures of effectiveness that allow for accurate and timely monitoring of essential services and infrastructure projects?

a. Major US military deployments in response to natural and man-made crises carry with them a very high political profile. Because of this, the need for information on progress is pervasive and must be provided to a wide range of audiences based on their interests in the crisis:

(1) **US Administration** – progress on meeting US mission objectives.

(2) **US Congress** – adherence to decisions reached in Congress; reporting to constituency.

(3) **News Media** – reporting news stories that meet the media's commercial objectives.

(4) **US Population** – US responsiveness to save lives and reduce human suffering has been a major interest to the US population – a fundamental part of our value system.

(5) **Coalition Partner Governments** – they are obliged to report to their populations the results of the interventions and their correspondence to national interests.

(6) **International Organizations** – The UN, the World Bank, UNHCR and other organizations also participate in crisis response, and are obliged to report progress to their member governments.

(7) **Global Populations** – crisis responses are of interest to different population groups relative to the various popular and political opinion trends that exist in different parts of the world.

b. The formulation of public affairs information as it flows to the various audiences is not the responsibility of the ES&CI project managers. However, understanding the constant demands from superiors and visitors for information in various forms is an important responsibility. The demands are often overwhelming; and determining when, exactly, time from project activities can be taken to accommodate the requests requires good judgment. Offers to send metrics teams to assist field managers are the most difficult to handle. They are usually not helpful because they take so much time from the field managers to learn the operations, only to conclude that they can't improve on the information already being provided. One technique in responding to requests for assistance is to simply state that the quantitative information is being collected adequately, and ask how the metrics team can help with the qualitative metrics (see below for a discussion on qualitative measures).

c. A common constraint to Phases IV and V reconstruction activities is the limited staff that is available and assigned to design, plan, and manage the activities. The USACE is supporting a range of research and development programs to develop information technology tools to increase efficiency of response effort in the field (e.g., managing reach-back support to expertise in the US or elsewhere on critical issues during field operations). USACE can be contacted to learn what tools are available, and their state of development. Researching metrics options is one type of external assistance that merits serious consideration. In particular, the manner in which qualitative measures can be formulated, training provided for HN authorities, and information systems to provide data can be one type of reach-back assistance that could be valuable.

2. Establish Baseline Data

a. **General**. Measuring progress is most successfully done by comparing current values with pre-crisis data. It is therefore important to get as much pre-crisis baseline data as possible, and to carefully select the data that is useful for the ES&CI project activities. Many countries have government offices that collect and report data for various purposes. To the extent that data is valid, it could be very useful as baseline data. However, one must be aware that some countries will issue biased reports for political purposes. Any un-analyzed HN data should be used with appropriate circumspection.

b. **Human Development Indicators (HDI)**

"The HDI is the original and best-known human development composite index. It is a summary measure of a country's average achievement in attaining:

a. A long and healthy life (as measured by life expectancy at birth);

b. Access to knowledge (today measured by two indicators: the adult literacy rate and the combined gross enrolment ratio (GER) in primary, secondary and tertiary education);

c. A decent standard of living (as measured by the gross domestic product (GDP) per capita expressed in purchasing power parity in US dollars)."[30]

(1) International organizations, such as the World Bank and the UNDP, also collect and report country-specific statistics. These reports would generally be very

useful as a source for baseline data. UNDP's HDI report (http://hdr.undp.org/en/statistics/) can be very useful. It is important to note, however, that between the international organization reports and data available from national government data services, the international organization reports are aggregate national data; while national government sources may break the data down by regions and cities.

(2) The HDI list is extensive. A quick review of the list will show that its emphasis is very much aligned around public health, economic and social system measurements that have little direct reference to either essential services or the infrastructure sector. But there are also available as baseline data several HDI measures that may be useful for this handbook sector, including:

> (a) cellular subscribers (per 1000 people);

> (b) electricity consumption per capita (% change);

> (c) electricity consumption per capita (kilowatt-hours);

> (d) electrification rate (%);

> (e) gas (as % of total primary energy supply);

> (f) nuclear power (as % of total primary energy supply);

> (g) oil (as % of total primary energy supply);

> (h) telephone mainlines (per 1000 people); and

> (i) total primary energy supply (TPES) (Mt of oil equivalent).

c. **The Sphere Project**

(1) Baseline data that can be used in infrastructure construction design and management to support the restoration of essential services can also come from the HA community. The Sphere Project – the Humanitarian Charter and Minimum Standards in Disaster Response[31] (http://www.sphereproject.org/) – is one commonly used reference by the HA community. (UNHCR also lists standards which are incorporated into the Sphere handbook).

(2) In the case above, the "minimum" standards are exactly that – the minimum requirements for sustaining life. For planners, the design of water, heat, shelter and health facilities can be based on such "minimum" standards rather than the normal criteria of projected demand. However, populations in general use resources far beyond the minimum requirements to sustain life, and normal demand projections are more commonly used as design criteria. The determination to use demand vs. minimum standards to design infrastructure will depend on resource availability, local expectations, and the larger political environment; both on site and in the donor community.

THE SPHERE PROJECT

This project provides standards for water/sanitation/hygiene, food security/
nutrition, shelter and health. Examples of "minimum standards" contained in
the Sphere handbook for one person's water requirements:

    a. For drinking and food – 2.5-3 liters/day

    b. For basic hygiene – 2-6 liters/day

    c. For cooking – 3-6 liters/day

    d. Total personal daily minimum – 7.5-15 liters/day.

---

    d. **Using Defense Critical Infrastructure Program (DCIP) Checklists**. The DCIP
assessment checklists provided in Appendix B will provide planners with a comprehensive
baseline infrastructure assessment from which to design project requirements, and measure
changes as the project matures. Per the DCIP introduction in subparagraph 4e(1) of
Chapter II, it is important here to reiterate that these checklists are derived from 1st World,
CONUS-like standards for construction and management. Planners must be particularly
careful to adapt them only after setting correct management conditions for the particular
utility or sector, and aligning expectations for the local environment.

3. Key Performance Indicators: Qualitative Metrics

    a. The determination of how progress is measured, and eventually mission success,
has become complex because of the nature of adversaries. Adversaries are not just
enemies in combat, but include the harshness of the environment in which the work is
being done. The conflict environment includes criminality, weak HN capacity, corruption,
and even imperfect cooperation among partners. Planners' natural tendencies are to seek
quantitative measures that are easy to collect and report. The greater challenge is to
identify relevant qualitative measures that show that the HN is performing its role
effectively to assure that the conditions that caused the conflict are not re-established.
In the case of steady-state Phase 0 operations, stabilization requires correcting the
conditions that could lead to crisis.

    b. **Measuring Progress in Conflict Environments (MPICE)**

*"There has been a longstanding need for "Measures of Effectiveness," as they are
often called in the private sector, focused on diplomatic, military and development
efforts in places prone to conflict. Traditionally, US Government agencies have
tended to measure outputs, such as the number of schools built, miles of roads
paved, or numbers of insurgents killed. Outputs, however, measure what we do
and not what we achieve. Outcomes, or "effects" as they are known in the military's
glossaries, indicate the success or failure of project or mission efforts, since they
seek to measure the attainment of conditions that engender stability and self-
sustaining peace."* [32]

(1) Outcomes can be both quantitative and qualitative. The quantity of electrical production in Iraq is a quantitative outcome that is seen as highly significant. Providing portable generator sets to hospitals in the interim period before central electrical production is reliable is an important quantitative measure. But equally important is to somehow measure of the capacity of the HN technical staff and the managers of the power generation sector to both maintain the restored infrastructure and to collect cost-recovery user fees in a transparent manner. Those are the difficult qualitative measures that also must be systematically obtained.

(2) An excerpt of the MPICE in Appendix C (slightly edited for clarity) lists examples of qualitative metrics. The full MPICE may be located at: http://handle.dtic.mil/100.2/ADA488249.

c. **Other Sources of Assessment Data**. Planners can derive appropriate metrics from a number of unconventional sources. For example, the Interagency Strategic Plan (developed by S/CRS) will list objectives, tasks, and sub-tasks under the MMEs/LOOs. Each task and sub-task will contain measures that will be used to determine progress and task achievement. Whatever sources the planner eventually chooses, the metrics must not be accepted simply because they are easy to collect. It is far more important that they are aligned with the national strategic end state and reflect careful judgment regarding the full scope of the project.

Intentionally Blank

APPENDIX A
DEFENSE CRITICAL INFRASTRUCTURE PROGRAM
ASSESSMENT CHECKLISTS

Derived from NSWC Assessment Checklists per Defense Critical Infrastructure Program (DCIP); (see DODI 3020.45 of April 21, 2008)

Note: The sectoral checklists below are re-formatted summaries of the full product found in DODI 3020.45 (series). The numbering schema in this appendix corresponds to the basic DOD instruction; any out-of-sequence numbering reflects editorial truncation of the primary text. The infrastructure assessment process here is defined in three parts: a) the standard; b) the benchmark(s) associated with that standard, and; c) specific questions related to that benchmark.

A.1. Energy- Electrical Power (EP)

The EP system network comprises primarily of substations, transmission lines, and power plants. These assets contain equipment, including transformers, circuit breakers, switches, and Supervisory Control and Data Acquisition (SCADA) systems. The primary goal of assessing the EP network is to ensure that the distribution network at a given location and the supporting off-site EP system hast the capacity, redundancy, path diversity, security survivability, and reliability to properly support its designated customers, community and/or region.

Assessment standards [shall] include:

- Standard 1. Maintain documents detailing the current configuration of the EP system that directly supports the customer (e.g., drawings, maps, blueprints, and schematics).

- Standard 2. Determine if the EP system has the ability to meet current and identified EP needs, including capacity, redundancy, path diversity and reliability, etc.

- Standard 3. Identify all system assets essential to supporting the continued and reliability delivery of EP to its customers.

- Standard 4. Maintain security to protect against threats and/or hazards commensurate with the needs and resources of all identified critical EP assets and identify the network's single points of failure (SPFs) if applicable.

- Standard 5. Maintain mitigation options and plans to eliminate or reduce the potential impact to a community in the event of an EP system disruption with the appropriate government and commercial EP suppliers and on-site operators and maintainers (e.g., backup generators, uninterruptible power supplies (UPSs), or redundant feeds, etc.) and identify the network's SPFs if applicable.

- Standard 6. Conduct routine preventive maintenance and testing of EP system components to ensure that the system remains in a reliable and safe condition to preclude operational failure resulting from natural degradation (e.g., spare parts, maintenance personnel, etc.).

Standard 1. Maintain documents detailing the current configuration of the EP system that directly supports the customer (e.g., drawings, maps, blueprints, and schematics).

Benchmark 1.1. Review the site's EP drawings, maps, blueprints, and schematics to answer the following:

Question 1.1.1. Are maps, drawings, schematics, or blueprints maintained and available that show network component locations, connections, operational/design parameters, access points, network control systems, etc. YES / NO

If YES, request copies Geographic Information Systems (GIS) or Computer-aided Design (CAD) drawings are the preferred formats.

If NO, skip to Benchmark 2.1.

Question 1.1.2. Are the major EP system components (e.g., power generation equipment, power distribution network, substations, and backup generators, etc.) identified in the drawings? YES / NO

Question 1.1.3. Are the documents current as of the date of the assessment? YES / NO

If NO, when were they last updated?

Question 1.1.4. Are any of these maps necessary for mission completion? YES / NO

If YES, answer Questions 1.1.4.1 and 1.1.4.2.

1.1.4.1. Has this information been protected, not been made available to the public, and kept in a secure onsite location? YES / NO

1.1.4.2. Is there a duplicate copy of these documents/drawings backed up and kept in a physically different site or location? YES / NO

Standard 2. Determine if the EP system has the ability to meet current and identified future EP needs (e.g., capacity, redundancy, path diversity, and reliability, etc.).

Benchmark 2.1. Identify system requirements for each function that requires EP and define what is an unacceptable loss of power. (if available, this information should be obtained from [the mission analyst][a city manager]).

Question 2.1.2. How long can the community or region go without EP before it begins to show signs of social or economic decay (identify interruption tolerance)?

Question 2.1.3. What is the normal and peak electric load of the community (for maximum and/or peak loads, consider surge and seasonal requirements)?

Benchmark 2.2. Define the site's electricity service provider and electrical power service by answering the following:

Question 2.2.1. Who is the electricity service provider (name and address) serving the site?

Question 2.2.2. Who is the electricity service provider's point of contact (POC) (provide the POC's name, office address, phone number, and email address)?

Question 2.2.3. Who is the commercial carrier that services the site (provide the commercial carrier's name, office address, phone number, and email address)?

Question 2.2.4. What type of contract does the site have with the service provider (firm (non-interruptible), standard, interruptible, or priority restoration)?

Question 2.2.5. What is the peak total distribution service load for the site (For maximum/ peak loads, consider surge requirements and or seasonal/weather requirements)?

Question 2.2.6. What is the primary distribution voltage of the site?

Benchmark 2.3. Define the onsite electricity service owner/operator by answering the following: (If the owner is the same as the provider, list in remarks and proceed to Benchmark 2.4.).

Question 2.3.1. Who is the onsite EP infrastructure owner (name and address)?

Question 2.3.2. Does the site have an emergency provisions contract with the EP system owner? YES / NO

If YES, describe.

Question 2.3.3. Does the owner subcontract any services (e.g., maintenance, emergency response, etc.)?

Benchmark 2.4. Identify the EP assets essential to supplying commercial or host-nation EP to the community and region (if necessary to the building or neighborhood level).

Question 2.4.1. Identify all sources for EP to the community and region.

Question 2.4.2. For each identified customer that requires EP, determine the following:

2.4.2.1. What are the essential assets that serve commercial EP to the customer (Trace the EP system backwards from the customer through the distribution and transmission system until you find a redundant source of EP)?

Question 2.4.3. Repeat for each facility, distribution system, and transmission system (until a redundant point of service and all likely SPFs have been discovered).

Question 2.4.4. Define the site's Essential Power Transmission (if applicable) by answering the following:

2.4.4.1. Identify transmission back to redundant feeds from the transmission substation serving the distribution.

2.4.4.2. Identify any alternate transmission components serving the site.

Benchmark 2.5. Record the site's information/characteristics of all EP assets defined in Benchmark 2.4 by answering the following (If this information is available and current from the collected documentation in Standard 1, skip to Benchmark 2.6; otherwise, validate those portions NOT current on submitted documentation):

Question 2.5.1. Identify pad or pole-mounted transformers (e.g., name/identification, capacity in kVA, voltage in kV, loading in kVA (base and peak), geo-location (i.e., decimal latitude and longitude), and what it serves).

Question 2.5.2. Identify transmission or distribution lines (e.g., name/identification, capacity in A, and to and from substation).

Question 2.5.3. Record the required information for each substation and the following assets within each substation that are essential for supplying power to the community.

2.5.3.1. Identify the substation (e.g., name/identification, voltage in kV, capacity in kVA, loading in kVA (base and peak), bus configuration, and geographic location (i.e., decimal latitude and longitude)).

2.5.3.2. Identify the transformers within the substation and characteristics of each using Question 2.5.1.

2.5.3.3. Identify the circuit breakers/switchgear (e.g., name/identification, capacity in A, circuit it protects).

2.5.3.4. Identify the bus bar (e.g., name/identification, voltage in kV, and configuration).

2.5.3.5. Identify the control systems (e.g., name/identification, system type (SCADA), and other systems information).

2.5.3.6. Other: information on any equipment within the substation that is deemed essential to supplying commercial or host-nation EP to the community by the subject-matter expert (SME).

Question 2.5.4. Do any of the assets identified share right-of-ways with other infrastructures (e.g., telecommunications, road, rail, natural gas/petroleum, or other)?

Question 2.5.5. Is there physical diversity sufficient to mitigate a single incident that could deny the mission capability? YES / NO

If NO, describe.

Benchmark 2.6. Define the site's EP generation by answering the following: (If this information is available and current from the collected documentation in Standard 1, skip to Benchmark 2.7; otherwise, validate those portions NOT current on submitted documentation).

Question 2.6.1. Identify the primary sources of EP generation:

> *2.6.1.1.* Plant or generator name;
>
> *2.6.1.2.* Address;
>
> *2.6.1.3.* Geolocation (i.e., decimal latitude and longitude);
>
> *2.6.1.4.* Capacity (MW);
>
> *2.6.1.5.* Loading (base/peak in kVA).

Question 2.6.2. Identify the alternate sources of EP generation:

2.6.2.1. Plant or generator name;

2.6.2.2. Address;

2.6.2.3. Geolocation (i.e., decimal latitude and longitude);

2.6.2.4. Capacity (MW);

2.6.2.5. Loading (base/peak in kVA).

Question 2.6.3. Identify what percentage the service provider uses to generate electricity:

> *2.6.3.1.* % Coal;
>
> *2.6.3.2.* % Oil;
>
> *2.6.3.3.* % Gas;
>
> *2.6.3.4.* % Hydro;
>
> *2.6.3.5.* % Nuclear.

Standard 3. Identify all system assets essential to supporting the continued and reliable delivery of EP to communities and businesses.

Benchmark 3.1. Identify and characterize those elements of the EP system that provide direct support to the community by answering the following (NOTE: Repeat for EACH community that relies on EP):

Question 3.1.1. Identify the EP components that directly support communities and businesses and processes (power distribution components, transformers, switchgear, power generators, backup power systems, UPSs, power monitoring and control systems, and power quality devices).

Question 3.1.2. Is each critical load on a supportable looped circuit, or does it have a redundant feed? YES / NO

Question 3.1.3. Are there any customers (such as electronics) that require additional power conditioning? YES / NO

Evaluate quality of service requirements.

3.1.3.1. Provide the power conditioning systems are in place in the EP system for each critical load?

Benchmark 3.2. Determine if all SPFs, based on system design components for the EP system supporting the community and customers, have been identified.

Question 3.2.1. Have the owners of the EP system identified and recorded any SPFs for the EP system? YES / NO

If YES, include in your list of SPFs.

Question 3.2.2. Have the owners of the EP system identified remedies for the SPF vulnerabilities that may affect critical missions? YES / NO

If YES, describe.

Question 3.2.3. Is the EP system designed so no SPFs exist in paths linking system elements deemed critical to the operations of a network? YES / NO

With this design, two or more simultaneous failures or errors must occur at the same time to cause a service interruption? YES / NO

Question 3.2.4. Identify each of these EP system critical components and SPFs supporting the community.

Question 3.2.5. Where feasible, do EP providers, system operators, and equipment suppliers provide emergency response for supporting communities and business activities? YES / NO

Benchmark 3.3. Determine if any SPFs for the EP system's physical pathways have been previously identified.

Question 3.3.1. Do critical EP distribution routes have physical diversity? YES / NO

Question 3.3.2. Has the site ensured that networks built with redundancy are also built with geographic separation? YES / NO

Question 3.3.3. Where physical pathway SPFs have been identified, have resolutions been considered such as using multiple EP suppliers to provide diverse connectivity to an alternate location? YES / NO

Benchmark 3.4. Ensure that a proper cyber security assessment has been performed for all EP control systems. In the absence of a proper cyber security assessment, the following questions will help identify the level to which EP control systems are in use at the site/ facility. NOTE: Repeat for EACH EP monitoring and control system- if more than one- that supports a community or business.

Question 3.4.1. Is there an EP monitoring and control system (e.g., SCADA, etc.) onsite? YES / NO NOTE: If there is more than one EP monitoring and control system, identify the geolocation (i.e., decimal latitude and longitude) of each and which portions of the system, including the communities, they support.

Question 3.4.2. What communications mechanism does this monitoring and control system use (e.g., public switched network (PSN), radio, leased lines, fiber optics, satellite, microwave, or wireless)?

Question 3.4.3. Is this monitoring and control system protected from outside access such as open or public communications paths (e.g., Internet, phone line, or radio frequency)? YES / NO

Question 3.4.4. Who has access to the system?

   3.4.4.1. Describe what access control measures are in place?

Question 3.4.5. What is the software used for this monitoring and control system? YES / NO

Has it been patched or upgraded? YES / NO

If YES, Provide the system and current patch/upgrade version.

Question 3.4.6. Is the cyber security posture adequate to prevent unauthorized access? YES / NO

Question 3.4.7. Who designed, installed, and operates this monitoring and control system?

Question 3.4.8. Does the site have onsite or offsite operational and/or maintenance personnel (number) for the monitoring and/or control system? YES / NO

Question 3.4.9. What backup EP systems are in place for this monitoring and control system (type and duration capabilities)?

Question 3.4.10. What types of backup communications systems are in place for this monitoring and control system?

Question 3.4.11. Are EP system operators trained to perform the required operations without the use of the monitoring and control system? YES / NO

Question 3.4.12. Have operations without this monitoring and control system been practiced or exercised within the last 12 months? YES / NO

Question 3.4.13. Does the site maintain replacement components or have appropriate contracts to ensure immediate response and repair for this monitoring and control system? YES / NO

If YES, list components.

Standard 4. Maintain security to protect against threats/hazards commensurate with the needs and resources of all identified critical EP assets and identify the network's single points of failure (SPFs) if applicable.

Benchmark 4.1. Determine the site's level of accessibility and security of the EP critical assets.

Question 4.1.1. Are the point-of-delivery substations that serve the site secured to prevent unauthorized access? YES / NO

Question 4.1.2. Identify who has access to each critical asset.

Question 4.1.3. Do all critical components of the site's EP system (except lines) restrict unauthorized access from the general population of the site, or are they buried to prevent unauthorized immediate access? YES / NO

Question 4.1.4. What portions of the EP system (except lines) have security features (i.e., video surveillance, intrusion detection systems, or fire suppression, etc.)? Describe existing security measures.

Question 4.1.5. Do site security agents regularly check the security of external portions of the EP system to detect attempts of unauthorized access? YES / NO

Question 4.1.6. Are all SPFs and critical elements of the site's EP system protected by access control measures to prevent unauthorized access? YES / NO

Question 4.1.7. Would any attempt to interrupt EP flow to critical assets on this site be detected? YES / NO

Benchmark 4.2. Determine the site's susceptibility level of the EP system to chemical, biological, radiological, and nuclear (CBRN) and electromagnetic pulse (EMP) events.

Benchmark 4.3. Determine the site's susceptibility level of the EP critical assets to explosion/sabotage or projectile impact effects.

Question 4.3.1. Do Explosive Ordnance Disposal (EOD) personnel have training or contingency plans for dealing with threats near EP system elements? YES / NO

If YES, describe.

Question 4.3.2. Are the EP system operators and maintenance personnel trained in procedures of what to do if they find suspicious packages near EP system elements? YES / NO

Question 4.3.3. Have EOD and EP systems operators and maintenance personnel practiced or exercised operations in EOD removal near EP systems within the past 12 months? YES / NO

Question 4.3.4. Identify those locations and key elements of the site's EP system that are observable to offsite locations (apartments, offices, and roads, etc.).

Question 4.3.5. Does hunting take place within 1 mile of the EP asset? YES / NO

Benchmark 4.4. Determine the site's susceptibility level of the EP system to cyber threats.

Question 4.4.1. Which elements of the EP monitoring and control system are electronically accessible to the outside world?

Question 4.4.2. Have those key EP systems with computer automation been subjected to a cyber threat evaluation? YES / NO

If YES, describe the evaluation.

Question 4.4.3. What were the identified vulnerabilities to automated EP system components by this inspection?

Question 4.4.4. Are systems protected against electromagnetic interference (EMI)? YES / NO

Question 4.4.5. Are systems protected against radio frequency interference (RFI)? YES / NO

Question 4.4.6. Are systems protected against energy-particle disruption? YES / NO

Question 4.4.7. Are systems protected against signal jamming? YES / NO

Question 4.4.8. Is information important to security protected from the public to include encryption of stored data? YES / NO

Question 4.4.9. Is information important to security protected from the public to include encryption of communications? YES / NO

Question 4.4.10. Identify and describe the corrective measures and quantitatively report the estimated reduction in vulnerability that has been put into place to mitigate these cyber vulnerabilities.

Benchmark 4.5. Determine the site's susceptibility level of to arson.

Question 4.5.1. Are any components of the EP system an attractive target for or unusually susceptible to arson (large stores of combustibles, etc.)? YES / NO

Question 4.5.2. Identify these locations that are attractive or susceptible to arson.

Benchmark 4.6. Determine the site's historical level of the EP system interference to intentional or accidental man-made damage mechanism events.

Question 4.6.1. Has the site ever experienced EP system outages? YES / NO

If YES, describe what caused the outage, how often did the outages occur, and what were the durations of the outages?

Question 4.6.2. Identify the average number of outages (and source of the outage) this has caused the site in the last 5 years.

Benchmark 4.7. Determine the site's susceptibility of the EP system elements that support communities to natural disasters (earthquakes, hurricanes, fire, and weather effects heat, cold, wind, etc.).

Question 4.7.1. Identify those key EP system components susceptible to damaging wind effects up to normal area maximums (provide the component name, identification, and wind speed and/or duration limitations).

Question 4.7.2. Identify those key EP system components susceptible to blowing debris (provide the component name, identification, and predicted wind speed and/or duration limitations).

Question 4.7.3. Are trees or other standing objects located far enough from EP system components that, if they fell, they would not impact the EP system? YES / NO

Question 4.7.4. Based on Questions 4.7.1 through 4.7.3, what is the lowest wind speed at which mission-impacting damage begins to occur to the EP system components (provide component name, identification, and wind speed)?

Question 4.7.5. Are key EP system components protected from electrical surge or lightning strike? YES / NO

Question 4.7.6. Which EP system components are vulnerable to damage from electrical surge and/or lightning effects, and at what level of voltage will this damage occur (provide component name, identification, and voltage level)?

Question 4.7.7. Are key EP system components protected from rain, water, and flooding effects? YES / NO

Question 4.7.8. Which EP system components are vulnerable to water damage (provide component name, identification, and describe the reason)?

Question 4.7.9. Are key EP system components protected from environmental heat and humidity effects? YES / NO

Question 4.7.10. Which EP system components are vulnerable to heat damage (provide component name, identification, and describe the reason)?

Question 4.7.11. Describe the tolerances of the EP system's components to heat and humidity (not fire) effects (e.g., temperature and humidity level at which operations are disrupted or fail).

Question 4.7.12. Are key EP system components resistant to cold and icing effects? YES / NO

Question 4.7.13. Which EP system components are vulnerable to cold and icing damage (provide component name, identification, and describe the reason)?

Question 4.7.14. Describe the tolerances of the EP system components to cold and icing effects (e.g., temperature or weight of ice at which asset fails or operations are disrupted).

Question 4.7.15. Are key EP system components protected from hail damage? YES / NO

Question 4.7.16. Which EP system components are vulnerable to hail damage (provide component name, identification, and describe the reason)?

Question 4.7.17. Describe the hail size that would cause critical damage to EP system components (e.g., any hail, ¾ to 1, 1 to 1½, or larger than 1½ inch, etc.).

Question 4.7.18. Are key EP system components resistant to snow accumulation? YES / NO

Question 4.7.19. Which EP system components are vulnerable to snow accumulation (provide component name, identification, and describe the reason)?

Question 4.7.20. Describe the tolerances of the EP system components to snow accumulation (e.g., feet of snow accumulation in a 24-hour period that would cause operations to be disrupted or fail).

Question 4.7.21. Is the site located outside areas where unique events such as tsunamis, earthquakes, mudslides, forest fires, or dam failures may occur? YES / NO

If YES, skip to Question 4.7.25.

Question 4.7.22. Which unique condition is the site located near?

Question 4.7.23. Does the site maintain contingency plans that address any possible unique event to that location? YES / NO

Question 4.7.24. Does the site maintain a capability of informing personnel and organizations of potentially dangerous weather conditions?
YES/NO

If YES, using what methods? How quickly? Time to inform?)

Question 4.7.25. Are EP system operators and maintenance personnel trained in procedures for operating during dangerous weather conditions? YES / NO

Question 4.7.26. Have EP system operators and maintenance personnel practiced or exercised operations in performing duties during dangerous weather within the past 12 months? YES / NO

Benchmark 4.8. Determine the site's susceptibility level of the EP system to fire.

Question 4.8.1. Does a certified Fire Inspector inspect the EP system, at least annually?
YES/NO

Question *4.8.2.* Are the identified hazards of fire inspections regularly tracked until all corrective actions have been taken? YES / NO

Question 4.8.3. Are fire-suppression systems available by all components of the EP system? YES / NO

   4.8.3.1. How long does it take to access fire-suppression systems?

Question 4.8.4. Are emergency breathing devices available to assist EP system personnel in fire suppression or evacuation? YES / NO

How many devices are needed? How many are on hand?

Question 4.8.5. Does an emergency lighting capability exist to assist EP system personnel in fire suppression or evacuation? YES / NO

Is the level of lighting adequate? YES / NO

If NO, describe.

Question 4.8.6. Are all EP system operators and maintenance personnel trained in fire-response activities? YES / NO

Question 4.8.7. Are responding fire-fighter personnel trained and equipped for dealing with EP system fires? YES / NO

Question 4.8.8. Can the EP system's supply be continued regardless of where a fire may occur? YES / NO

   4.8.8.1. Which elements of the EP system, if on fire, would cause disruption of EP system (provide component name, identification, geolocation (i.e., decimal latitude and longitude, and level of interruption (full or partial)))?

Question 4.8.9. Have EP system operators, maintenance, and fire-response personnel practiced or exercised fire response on the EP system within the past 12 months? YES / NO

Benchmark 4.9. Determine the site's susceptibility level of the EP system to other natural or accidental threats.

Question 4.9.1. Is all construction and digging onsite coordinated through a single office and capable of comparing the dig location to that of EP system elements? YES / NO

Question 4.9.2. Is the site's EP system susceptible to mission failure due to work stoppage or strike? YES / NO

Identify appropriate groups or unions.

Question 4.9.3. Is the site's EP system susceptible to mission failure due to animal activity (susceptibility)? YES / NO

Standard 5. Maintain mitigation options and plans to eliminate or reduce the potential impact to a community in the event of a power system disruption with the appropriate government and commercial EP suppliers and onsite operators and/or maintainers (e.g., backup generators, uninterruptible power supplies (UPSs), or redundant feeds, etc.) and identify the network's SPF if applicable.

Benchmark 5.1. Review EP-related contingency plans to answer the following:

Question 5.1.1. Does the site maintain a contingency plan to ensure availability of the EP network to accomplish its mission? YES / NO

If NO, skip to Question 5.1.2.

   5.1.1.1. Is the plan operationally feasible and logistically supportable? YES / NO

   5.1.1.2. Are the necessary personnel required to implement these plans available to respond onsite at all times? YES / NO

   5.1.1.3. Has the plan been protected and not released to the public? YES / NO

   5.1.1.4. What date was the plan last reviewed and updated?

   5.1.1.5. What date was the plan last exercised?

5.1.1.6. Does this plan enlist external parties (service provider, etc.)? YES / NO

5.1.1.7. Has this plan been coordinated and signed by the external parties? YES / NO

5.1.1.8. Have there been any difficulties in getting these units when needed? YES / NO

Question 5.1.2. Are emergency drills performed to test the site's ability to alternately route EP supplies to DCAs? YES / NO

Question 5.1.3. Has the site's ability to alternately route EP supplies to DCAs been tested? YES / NO

Question 5.1.4. Is a switching capability available to drop non-critical loads in support of other critical loads? YES / NO

5.1.4.1. Is there a plan in place to facilitate this load-shedding? YES / NO

Benchmark 5.2. Identify if backup power generation to support community requirements has been considered by answering the following (NOTE: Repeat for EACH community that relies on EP):

Question 5.2.1. For each DCA that relies on EP, is emergency backup power capability available (i.e., backup generation available for each community and/or business requirement)? YES / NO

Question 5.2.2. Are those communities or businesses that cannot afford a temporary loss of power or that require a continuous flow of clean power connected to an UPS? YES / NO

5.2.2.1. Can the UPS maintain COOP for the prescribed time limit for their loads until the primary or backup power is restored? YES / NO

Question 5.2.3. If the primary power is disrupted, can backup EP sources (e.g., UPS, generators, etc.) meet the demand of all required functions? YES / NO NOTE: reference power requirements from Standard 2.

Question 5.2.4. Can the backup power be sustained for the required amount of time to complete the mission, primary service restored, or relocation of mission? YES / NO

Question 5.2.5. How long can backup systems sustain a COOP for critical operations (including provisions for sustained operations, oil, fuel, spare parts, or maintenance, etc.)?

Question 5.2.6. Are support personnel notified when commercial EP is lost (e.g., indicator and monitoring lights, etc.) so that a power outage is not mistaken for a power surge? YES / NO

Question 5.2.7. Do the backup generators have automatic startup capability if commercial EP is lost? YES / NO

Question 5.2.8. Are the trained maintenance, technical, and operations staffs available to operate and maintain the EP system during normal, backup, emergency, and no EP scenarios? YES / NO

Question 5.2.9. Describe how the backup generators are refueled.

Question 5.2.10. Does the site maintain sufficient quantities of the proper fuels to refuel backup generators? YES / NO

Question 5.2.11. Does the site maintain mobile electrical power supplies (MEPS) or non-dedicated generators that can be used by the community? YES / NO

If NO, do they have a resource to obtain them?

Question 5.2.12. Has a Standing Operating Procedure (SOP) been developed for priority use of site MEPS or non-dedicated generators? YES / NO

Standard 6. Conduct routine preventive maintenance and testing of EP system components to ensure that the system remains in a reliable and safe condition to preclude operational failure, resulting from natural degradation (e.g., spare parts, maintenance personnel, etc.).

Benchmark 6.1. Determine if the site's routine preventive maintenance and testing of EP system components is sufficient for mission assurance. NOTE: Repeat for each community that relies on EP.

Question 6.1.1. Does the site perform routine preventive and corrective maintenance of the EP system? YES / NO

Question 6.1.2. Are periodic surge/emergency operations and end-to-end drills conducted to test the EP distribution's primary and/or backup systems under full-demand conditions? YES / NO

Question 6.1.3. Does an established, documented preventive maintenance program support the backup EP systems? YES / NO

Question 6.1.4. Are the backup generators operated or tested under load to verify operations? YES / NO

If YES, how often are the tests conducted?

Question 6.1.5. Are UPS units regularly monitored and tested? YES / NO

Question 6.1.6. Are all site operators and maintainers available to respond onsite at all times? YES / NO

Question 6.1.7. Identify those skill sets or positions where only one individual is capable of performing operational or maintenance duties.

<u>Benchmark 6.2.</u> Determine if the site maintains sufficient component inventories, part replacement contingencies, maintenance personnel, expertise, and contingency plans to guarantee mission accomplishment.

Question 6.2.1. Does the site conduct EP system component inventories?

Question 6.2.2. Are sufficient spare parts and consumables available to meet the endurance limitations of backup systems to correct casualties to primary EP systems supporting critical missions?

Standard 7. Identify dependencies on and support provided to other SFINs.

<u>Benchmark 7.1.</u> Identify dependencies on and support provided to other SFINs.

Question 7.1.1. Does the EP system require petroleum to operate? YES / NO

If YES, provide the reason.

　　7.1.1.1. What is the primary source and mode of delivery?

　　7.1.1.2. What are the alternative or redundant sources?

Question 7.1.2. Does the EP system require natural gas to operate? YES / NO

If YES, provide the reason.

　　7.1.2.1. What is the primary source and mode of delivery?

　　7.1.2.2. What are the alternative/redundant sources?

Question 7.1.3. Does the EP system require any communications systems to operate? YES / NO

If YES, provide the reason.

Question 7.1.4. Does the EP system require any road transportation to operate? YES / NO

If YES, provide the reason.

Question 7.1.5. Does the EP system require any rail transportation to operate? YES / NO

If YES, provide the reason.

Question 7.1.6. Does the EP system require any aviation transportation to operate? YES / NO

If Yes, describe and provide the reason.

Question 7.1.7. Does the EP system require any maritime transportation to operate? YES / NO

If YES, provide the reason.

Question 7.1.8. Does the EP system require any HVAC to operate? YES / NO

If YES, provide the reason.

Question 7.1.9. Does the EP system require any water to operate? YES / NO

If YES, provide the reason.

Question 7.1.10. Does the EP system require any chemicals to operate? YES / NO

If YES, provide the reason.

Question 7.1.11. Have any other dependencies or interdependencies for EP been identified? YES / NO

If YES, describe.

STOP: **If you answered YES for any of 7.1.1 through 7.1.11, ensure that you accomplish the benchmark for that area.**

A.2. Energy- Natural Gas

Natural gas networks downstream from producing wells and gathering systems comprise processing plants, liquefied natural gas terminals, gasification and degasification plants, and transmission and distribution pipeline systems. Natural gas is transported from production and processing facilities over transmission pipelines to distribution pipelines located throughout a local distribution company's (LDC) service area. Transmission pipeline systems include market center hubs, compressor stations, storage facilities, city gates, and interconnection points. Distribution pipeline systems include storage facilities, meter stations, and compressed natural gas terminals. LDCs receive natural gas through city gates to a system of distribution pipelines that supply gas to individual customers' meters. The primary goal of assessing the natural gas network is to ensure that the distribution network at a given location and the supporting offsite natural gas system has the capacity, redundancy, path diversity, security, survivability, and reliability to properly support a particular region or community.

- <u>STANDARD 1.</u> Maintain documents detailing the current configuration of the natural gas system that directly supports the community (e.g., drawings, maps, blueprints, and schematics).

- <u>STANDARD 2.</u> Determine if the natural gas system has the ability to meet current and identified future natural gas needs of the region or community (e.g., capacity, redundancy, path diversity, and reliability, etc.).

- <u>STANDARD 3.</u> Identify all system assets essential to supporting the continued and reliable delivery of natural gas to the region or community.

- <u>STANDARD 4.</u> Maintain security to protect against threats/hazards commensurate with the needs and resources of all identified critical natural gas assets. Department of Defense (DOD) Components may consider working with the commercial or municipal entities owning natural gas delivery equipment and installations to enhance security on a case-by-case basis.

- <u>STANDARD 5.</u> Maintain mitigation options and plans to eliminate or reduce the potential impact to a mission in the event of a natural gas supply disruption with appropriate government and commercial natural gas distributors and onsite owner-operators (e.g., storage facilities, looped distribution systems, and secondary service meters, etc.) and identify the network's single points of failure (SPFs) if applicable.

- <u>STANDARD 6.</u> Conduct routine preventive maintenance and testing of natural gas system components to ensure that the system remains in a reliable and safe condition to preclude operational failure, resulting from natural degradation (e.g., spare parts, maintenance personnel, etc.).

- <u>STANDARD 7.</u> Identify dependencies on and support provided to other SFINs.

APPLICABILITY TEST:

(1) Does the community use natural gas products? YES / NO

(2) Will the lack of these natural gas products prevent or negatively impact the community or local and regional businesses? YES / NO

(3) Are elements of natural gas control, usage, or storage located within 500 feet of any identified critical or DOD mission assets? YES / NO

STOP: If you answered YES to any of the questions (1-2), continue to Benchmark 1.1. If you answered YES ONLY to question (3), ensure you list natural gas as a potential hazard to mission assets and stop processing these benchmarks. If you answered NO to questions (1-3), you may skip processing these benchmarks.

Standard 1. Maintain documents detailing the current configuration of the natural gas system that directly supports the region or community (e.g., drawings, maps, blueprints, and schematics).

Benchmark 1.1. Review site natural gas drawings, maps, blueprints, and schematics to answer the following:

Question 1.1.1. Are maps, drawings, schematics, or blueprints maintained and available that show network component locations, connections, operational/design parameters, access points, and network control systems, etc. (ArcMap shape files, Computer Aided Design (CAD) drawings, and Geographical Information System (GIS) are the preferred formats)? YES / NO

If YES, request copies in the preferred formats.

If NO, skip to Benchmark 2.1.

Question 1.1.2. Are the major natural gas system components identified in the drawings (e.g., compressors, pumps, storage facilities, and receipt or delivery points)? YES / NO

If YES, identify each component.

Question 1.1.3. Are the documents current as of the date of the assessment? YES / NO

If NO, when were they last updated?

Question 1.1.4. Has this information been protected, not been made available to the public, and kept in a secure onsite location? YES / NO

Question 1.1.5. Are any of the maps necessary for mission completion? YES / NO

If YES, answer Question 1.1.6.

Question 1.1.6. Are duplicate copies of these documents or drawings backed up offsite? YES / NO

STOP: Collect/submit any electronic copies of these documents with your final data for database review.

Standard 2. Determine if the natural gas system has the ability to meet current and identified future natural gas needs of the region and community (e.g., capacity, redundancy, path diversity, reliability, etc.).

Benchmark 2.1. Describe the site's relationship with the LDC by answering the following:

Question 2.1.1. Identify the LDC that serves the site (provide company name, company address, and telephone numbers).

Question 2.1.2. Who are the LDCs' points of contact (POCs)? Identify POC by office symbol, office name, and telephone numbers.

Question 2.1.3. What are the contract-stipulated quantities of natural gas that the site has with the LDC, any other natural gas providers, or storage sites? Identify by name and contracted quantity for distribution.

Question 2.1.4. What is the transmission company's priority for natural gas service to the LDC compared to other LDCs? Identify the priority of service offered by this LDC vs. the priority offered by other LDCs.

Question 2.1.5. What is the LDC's priority for natural gas service to this site compared to other natural gas customers? Identify by name or type, those customers the LDC places ahead of the site (e.g., hospitals, residential customers, etc.).

Question 2.1.6. If there is a disruption from the natural gas supplier, does the transmission company or LDC have available natural gas and/or an alternative natural gas source? YES/NO

If YES, identify the company name and address.

Question 2.1.7. Is the site's natural gas network selected for privatization? YES / NO

If YES, has a contract (company and address) been awarded?

Benchmark 2.2. Defense Energy Support Center's relationship to the site (Deleted)

Benchmark 2.3. Describe the site's natural gas infrastructure owner by answering the following:

Question 2.3.1. Identify the natural gas infrastructure owner at the site (provide company name, company address, and telephone numbers).

Question 2.3.2. Who are the owner's POCs (provide POC by office symbol, office name, and telephone numbers)?

Question 2.3.3. Does the site have an emergency provisions contract with the natural gas providers? YES / NO

Question 2.3.4. Does the site receive priority restoration of natural gas deliveries? YES / NO.

If YES, describe.

Question 2.3.5. Does the owner subcontract any services (e.g., maintenance or lab services)? YES / NO

If YES, identify POC by office symbol, office name, and telephone numbers.

Benchmark 2.4. Describe the site's natural gas infrastructure operator by answering the following: (If the owner is the operator, skip to Benchmark 2.5.)

Question 2.4.1. Identify the natural gas system operator of the site (provide company name, company address, and telephone numbers).

Question 2.4.2. Who are the operator's POCs (provide POCs by office symbol, office name, and telephone numbers)?

Question 2.4.3. Does the site have an emergency provisions contract with the natural gas providers? YES / NO

Question 2.4.4. Does the site receive priority restoration of natural gas deliveries? YES / NO

If YES, describe

Question 2.4.5. Does the operator subcontract any services (e.g., maintenance or lab services)? YES / NO

If YES, identify POC by office symbol, office name, and telephone numbers.

Benchmark 2.5. Define the natural gas processing facility that may serve the region or community by answering the following:

Question 2.5.1. Identify what natural gas process plants provide the service provider natural gas. Provide plant name, address, geolocation (i.e., decimal latitude and longitude), and total capacity in thousands of cubic feet per day (MCF/D).

Question 2.5.2. Who are the natural gas processing facilities' POCs (provide POCs by office symbol, name, title, and telephone numbers)?

Question 2.5.3. Identify the connected natural gas pipeline systems (name and receipt capacity MCF/D) to the natural gas processing facility.

Question 2.5.4. Identify alternate sources of natural gas processing for the site (provide plant name, address, geolocation (i.e., decimal latitude and longitude), and total capacity MCF/D.

Benchmark 2.6. Define the natural gas storage and peak shaving facilities that serve the site.

Question 2.6.1. Identify the natural gas storage and peak shaving facilities that may provide natural gas products to the site (provide plant name, address, geolocation (i.e., decimal latitude and longitude), and total capacity in MCF/D.

Question 2.6.2. Who are the natural gas storage and peak shaving facilities' POCs (provide POCs by office symbol, name, title, and telephone numbers)?

Question 2.6.3. Identify natural gas storage and peak shaving facilities storage components (tanks by number, type, underground or aboveground, and capacity in barrels).

Question 2.6.4. Identify the connected natural gas pipeline systems to the natural gas storage and peak shaving facilities (provide pipeline system name and receipt capacity in MCF/D)

Benchmark 2.7. Define the natural gas distribution to site.

Question 2.7.1. Identify primary distribution components to the site (e.g., storage, city gates, meter stations, compressor stations, and manifolds/valve boxes) (provide number, type, geolocation (i.e., decimal latitude and longitude), underground or aboveground, and capacity in MCF/D).

Question 2.7.2. Identify quantity of natural gas distributed to the site (capacity, peak and off-peak in MCF/D).

Question 2.7.3. Identify alternate distribution components (provide number, type, geolocation (i.e., decimal latitude and longitude), underground or above ground, and capacity in MCF/D).

Benchmark 2.8. If the site has a natural gas monitoring and/or control system (e.g., SCADA, etc.), answer the following; otherwise skip to Standard 3. NOTE: Repeat for EACH natural gas monitoring and/or control system, if more than one, which supports a DCA.

Question 2.8.1. Is there a natural gas monitoring and/or control system onsite? YES / NO

If YES, identify where it is located.

If NO, skip to Standard 3.

If there is more than one natural gas monitoring and/or control system, identify the geolocation (i.e., decimal latitude and longitude) of each and which portions of the system, including the DCAs, they support.

Question 2.8.2. What communications mechanisms does this monitoring and/or control system use (e.g., public switched network (PSN), radio, leased lines, fiber optics, satellite, or microwave)?

Question 2.8.3. What is the age of this monitoring and/or control system?

Question 2.8.4. On what type of platform does this monitoring and/or control system operate?

Question 2.8.5. Who designed, installed, and operates this monitoring and/or control system (provide organization, address, and contact number).

Question 2.8.6. Does the site have onsite or offsite operational and/or maintenance personnel for the monitoring and/or control system? YES / NO

If YES, list how many.

Question 2.8.7. How often are this system's operational parameters checked or monitored?

Question 2.8.8. Can the natural gas system supporting a critical mission or asset operate independently if this monitoring and/or control system is not operational? YES / NO

Question 2.8.9. What backup communications systems are in place for this monitoring and/or control system?

Question 2.8.10. Have operations without the monitoring and/or control system been practiced or exercised within the last 12 months? YES / NO

Question 2.8.11. Is this monitoring and/or control system protected from outside access such as open or public communications paths (e.g., Internet, phone line, or radio frequency)? YES / NO

If YES, identify the access points.

Question 2.8.12. Does the site maintain replacement components for the monitoring and/or control system or have appropriate contracts to ensure immediate response and repair? YES / NO

Standard 3. Identify all system assets essential to supporting the continued and reliable delivery of natural gas to region or communities.

Benchmark 3.1. Define the key elements of site data that support critical missions and processes by answering the following (NOTE: Repeat for each type):

Question 3.1.1. Does more than one natural gas feed supply the site? YES / NO

If YES, provide geolocation (i.e., decimal latitude and longitude) where each natural gas feed enters the site.

Question 3.1.2. Can a single natural gas feed supply all the natural gas needs for the critical and mission assets? YES / NO

If feed lines have different load capabilities, identify them

Question 3.1.3. Identify the natural gas pipeline components that are important to the site (e.g., compressors, storage facilities, and receipt and delivery points) (provide each type of component and its geolocation (i.e., decimal latitude and longitude)).

Question 3.1.4. What types of natural gas distribution systems are located onsite (provide system name, looped/dead-end, and meter identification with geolocation (i.e., decimal latitude and longitude))?

Question 3.1.5. What LDC and site service meters are connected to mission-required assets? Identify the each mission-required asset, associated LDC, and service meter.

Question 3.1.6. What is the estimated mission-related consumption, broken down by mission requirements, for average and peak day? Identify the total estimated daily consumption of natural gas by critical and mission assets and processes in MCF/D.

<u>Benchmark 3.2.</u> Identify if the site has backup natural gas products to support the mission by answering the following:

Question 3.2.1. Does the site have pre-positioned natural gas and/or alternative fuel inventories? YES / NO

Question 3.2.2. What natural gas substitution is available, if any, and for what facilities? Identify alternative (e.g., propane), quantity, facility, or not applicable.

Question 3.2.3. Where is the alternate fuel storage site (provide location by name, building number, and geolocation (i.e., decimal latitude and longitude), type of storage container, quantity stored by type of product, or not applicable)?

Question 3.2.4. Based on typical usage, how long will the reserves last (number of days/hours)?

Question 3.2.5. Are these fuel reserves monitored and inventoried? YES / NO

If YES, describe for each fuel type; e.g., local, remote, etc.

<u>Benchmark 3.3.</u> Describe the support the site's natural gas distribution system provides DCAs, as identified by mission requirements, by answering the following: (Repeat for each community that relies on Natural gas.)

Question 3.3.1. For each identified customer base, does that community or region have more than one natural gas supply point? YES / NO

Identify geolocation (i.e., decimal latitude and longitude) for each natural gas supply point entering the area and fuel type.

Question 3.3.2. For each community, what is the estimated peak consumption? Identify the total estimated daily consumption of natural gas (MCF or propane – gallons).

Question 3.3.3. Does the community have pre-positioned natural gas inventories? YES / NO

Question 3.3.4. Where is this inventory storage site (provide location by name, building number, geolocation (i.e., decimal latitude and longitude), type of storage container, quantity stored, or not applicable)?

Question 3.3.5. How long will the inventory sustain business-related or normal household activities (number of days or not applicable)?

Benchmark 3.4. Determine if all SPFs, based on system design components for the natural gas system supporting regions, communities or businesses, have been identified.

Question 3.4.1. Have the owners and/or operators of the natural gas system identified and recorded any SPF vulnerabilities of the system? YES / NO

Question 3.4.2. Identify each of these natural gas system critical components and SPFs supporting the community (provide each SPF by component, cause, and geolocation (i.e., decimal latitude and longitude)).

Question 3.4.3. Is the natural gas system designed so no SPFs exist in paths linking system elements deemed critical to the operations of a network (with this design, two or more simultaneous failures or errors must occur at the same time to cause a service interruption)? YES / NO

Question 3.4.4. Where feasible, do natural gas providers, system operators, and equipment suppliers provide emergency response for supporting the community? YES / NO

Question 3.4.5. Have the owners and/or operators of the natural gas system identified remedies for the SPF vulnerabilities that may affect critical services? YES / NO

Benchmark 3.5. Determine if all SPFs for the natural gas system's physical pathways have been identified.

Question 3.5.1. Do critical natural gas distribution routes have physical diversity (e.g., not co-located, not sharing rights-of-way, etc.)? YES / NO

. If NO, describe.

Question 3.5.2. Where physical pathway SPFs have been identified, have resolutions been considered, such as using multiple natural gas suppliers to provide diverse connectivity to an alternate location? YES / NO

Describe.

Standard 4. Maintain security to protect against threats/hazards commensurate with the needs and resources of all identified critical natural gas assets. DOD Components may find it necessary to work with the commercial or municipal entities owning natural gas delivery equipment and installations to enhance security on a case-by-case basis.

Benchmark 4.1. Determine the level of accessibility and security of the site's natural gas critical assets by answering the following:

Question 4.1.1. Are the natural gas delivery points that serve the site secured to prevent unauthorized access? YES / NO

Question 4.1.2. Identify by name and location who has access to each critical asset.

Question 4.1.3. Do all critical components of the natural gas system restrict unauthorized access from the general population, or are they buried to prevent unauthorized immediate access? YES / NO

Question 4.1.4. What portions of the natural gas system have security features (e.g., video surveillance, intrusion-detection systems, fire suppression, etc.)? Describe security measures.

Question 4.1.5. Do site security agents regularly check the security of external portions of the natural gas system to detect attempts of unauthorized access? YES / NO

Question 4.1.6. Are all SPFs and critical elements of the site's natural gas system protected by access control measures to prevent unauthorized access? YES / NO

Question 4.1.7. Would any attempt to interrupt or contaminate the natural gas flow be detected by the site? YES / NO

Benchmark 4.2. Determine the susceptibility level of the site's natural gas system to chemical, biological, radiological, nuclear, and explosive (CBRNE) events. (Deleted).

Benchmark 4.3. Determine the susceptibility level of the site's natural gas system to explosion/sabotage or projectile impact effects.

Question 4.3.1. Does the site have the capability to detect explosive threats in delivery vehicles or mail delivery? YES / NO

If YES, what are the threshold detection levels?

Question 4.3.2. Does the site have dedicated Explosive Ordnance Disposal (EOD) support? YES / NO

Question 4.3.3. Do EOD personnel have training or contingency plans for dealing with threats near natural gas system elements? YES / NO

Question 4.3.4. Are natural gas system operators and maintenance personnel trained in procedures of what to do if they find suspicious packages near natural gas system elements? YES / NO

Question 4.3.5. Have EOD and natural gas systems operators and maintenance personnel practiced or exercised operations in EOD removal near natural gas systems within the past 12 months? YES / NO

Question 4.3.6. Identify those locations and key elements (e.g., apartments, offices, roads, etc.) of the site's natural gas system that are observable to offsite locations? List geolocation (i.e., decimal latitude and longitude) and describe general degree window of observability.

Question 4.3.7. Does hunting take place within 1 mile of the site? YES / NO

Benchmark 4.4. Determine the susceptibility level of the site's natural gas system to cyber threats. NOTE: Repeat for all qualifying components.

Question 4.4.1. Which elements of the natural gas system are electronically accessible to the outside world (provide component name, identification, and describe accessibility (e.g., telephone line or modem, etc.)?

Question 4.4.2. Have those key natural gas systems with computer automation been subjected to a cyber threat evaluation? YES / NO

Describe the evaluation.

Question 4.4.3. What were the identified vulnerabilities to automated natural gas system components by this inspection?

Question 4.4.4. Are systems protected against electromagnetic interference (EMI)? YES / NO

Question 4.4.5. Are systems protected against radio frequency interference (RFI)? YES / NO

Question 4.4.6. Are systems protected against energy-particle disruption? YES / NO

Question 4.4.7. Are systems protected against signal jamming? YES / NO

Question 4.4.8. Is information important to security protected from the public to include encryption of stored data? YES / NO

Question 4.4.9. Is information important to security protected from the public to include encryption of communications? YES / NO

Question 4.4.10. Identify and describe the corrective measures and quantitatively report the estimated reduction in vulnerability that has been put into place to mitigate these cyber vulnerabilities

Benchmark 4.5. Determine the site's susceptibility level to arson.

Question 4.5.1. Are any components of the natural gas system an attractive target for or uniquely susceptible to arson (large stores of combustibles, etc.)? YES / NO

Question 4.5.2. Identify the locations that are attractive or susceptible to arson.

Benchmark 4.6. Determine the historical level of the site's natural gas system to intentional or accidental man-made damage mechanism events.

Question 4.6.1. Has the site ever experienced natural gas system outages? YES / NO

If YES, describe what caused the outage, how often the outages occurred, and what were the durations of the outages?

Question 4.6.2. Identify the average number of outages (and source of the outage) this has caused the site in the last 5 years.

Benchmark 4.7. Determine the susceptibility of the site's natural gas system elements that support DCAs to natural disasters (earthquakes, hurricanes, fire, and weather effects (heat, cold, wind, etc.)). Repeat for all system components.

Question 4.7.1. Identify those key natural gas system components susceptible to damaging wind effects up to normal area maximums (provide component name, identification, wind speed, and/or duration limitations).

Question 4.7.2. Identify those key natural gas system components susceptible to blowing debris (provide component name, identification, wind speed, and/or duration limitations).

Question 4.7.3. Are trees or other standing objects located far enough from natural gas system components that, if they fell, they would not impact the natural gas system? YES / NO

Question 4.7.4. Based on Questions 4.7.1 through 4.7.3, what is the lowest wind speed at which mission-impacting damage will begin to occur to the natural gas system components (provide component name, identification, and wind speed)?

Question 4.7.5. Are key natural gas system components protected from electrical surge or lightning strike? YES / NO

Question 4.7.6. Which natural gas system components are vulnerable to damage from electrical surge and/or lightning effects, and at what level of voltage will this damage occur (provide component name, identification, and voltage level).

Question 4.7.7. Are key natural gas system components protected from rain, water, and flooding effects? YES / NO

Question 4.7.8. Which natural gas system components are vulnerable to water damage (provide component name, identification, and describe the reason)?

Question 4.7.9. Describe the rain, water, and flooding conditions that would cause damage to natural gas system components (e.g., flash flooding, the approximate flooding depth at which damage would occur, etc.).

Question 4.7.10. Are key natural gas system components protected from heat and humidity (not fire) effects? YES / NO

Question 4.7.11. Which natural gas system components are vulnerable to heat damage (provide component name, identification, and describe the reason)?

Question 4.7.12. Describe the tolerances of the natural gas system's components to environmental heat and humidity (i.e., not fire) effects (e.g., temperature and humidity level at which operations are disrupted or fail).

Question 4.7.13. Are key natural gas system components resistant to cold and icing effects? YES / NO

Question 4.7.14. Which natural gas system components are vulnerable to cold and icing damage (provide component name, identification, and describe the reason)?

Question 4.7.15. Describe the tolerances of the natural gas system components to cold and icing effects (e.g., temperature or weight of ice at which asset fails or operations are disrupted).

Question 4.7.16. Are key natural gas system components protected from hail damage? YES / NO

Question 4.7.17. Which natural gas system components are vulnerable to hail damage (provide component name, identification, and describe the reason)?

Question 4.7.18. Describe the hail size that would cause critical damage to natural gas system components (e.g., any hail, ¾ to 1, 1 to 1½, or larger than 1½ inch, etc.).

Question 4.7.19. Are key natural gas system components resistant to snow accumulation? YES / NO

Question 4.7.20. Which natural gas system components are vulnerable to snow accumulation (provide component name, identification, and describe the reason)?

Question 4.7.21. Describe the tolerances of the natural gas system components to snow accumulation (e.g., feet of snow accumulation in a 24-hour period that would cause operations to be disrupted or fail).

Question 4.7.22. Is the site located outside areas where unique events such as tsunamis, earthquakes, mudslides, forest fires, or dam failures may occur? YES / NO

If YES, skip to Question 4.8.

Question 4.7.23. Describe which unique condition (per Q 4.7.22) the site is located near.

Question 4.7.24. Does the site maintain contingency plans that address any possible unique event to that location? YES / NO

Question 4.7.25. Does the site maintain a capability of informing personnel and organizations of potentially dangerous weather conditions? YES / NO

If YES, using what methods? How quickly? Time to inform?

Question 4.7.26. Are natural gas system operators and maintenance personnel trained in procedures for operating during dangerous weather conditions? YES / NO

Question 4.7.27. Have natural gas system operators and maintenance personnel practiced or exercised operations in performing duties during dangerous weather within the past 12 months? YES / NO

Benchmark 4.8. Determine the site's susceptibility level of the natural gas system to fire.

Question 4.8.1. Does a certified Fire Inspector inspect the site's natural gas system, at least annually? YES / NO

Question 4.8.2. Are the identified hazards of fire inspections regularly tracked until all corrective actions have been taken? YES / NO

Question 4.8.3. Are fire-suppression systems available by all components of the natural gas system? YES / NO?

If YES, how long does it take to access fire-suppression systems?

Question 4.8.4. Are emergency breathing devices available to assist natural gas system personnel in fire suppression or evacuation? YES / NO

If YES, how many devices are needed? How many are on hand?

Question 4.8.5. Does an emergency lighting capability exist to assist natural gas system personnel in fire suppression or evacuation? YES / NO

Is the level of lighting adequate? YES / NO

Question 4.8.6. Are all natural gas system operators and maintenance personnel trained in fire-response activities? YES / NO

Question 4.8.7. Are responding fire-fighter personnel trained and equipped for dealing with natural gas system fires? YES / NO

Question 4.8.8. Can the natural gas system's supply be continued regardless of where a fire may occur? YES / NO

If YES, proceed to Question 4.8.10.

Question 4.8.9. Which elements of the natural gas system, if on fire, would cause a disruption to the natural gas system (provide component name, identification, geolocation (i.e., decimal latitude and longitude), and level of interruption (full or partial)?

Question 4.8.10. Have natural gas system operators, maintenance, and fire-response personnel practiced or exercised fire response on the natural gas system within the past 12 months? YES / NO

Benchmark 4.9. Determine the site's susceptibility level of the natural gas system to other natural/accidental threats.

Question 4.9.1. Is all construction and digging onsite coordinated through a single office and capable of comparing location to that of natural gas system elements? YES / NO

Question 4.9.2. Is the site's natural gas system susceptible to mission failure due to work stoppage or strike? YES / NO

Identify appropriate groups or unions.

Question 4.9.3. Is the site's natural gas system susceptible to mission failure due to animal activity (susceptibility)? YES / NO

Benchmark 4.10. Determine the historical level of the site's natural gas system to natural disaster events.

Question 4.10.1. Has the site ever experienced natural gas system outages? YES / NO

If YES, describe what caused the outages, how often the outages occurred, and what were the durations of the outages?

Question 4.10.2. Identify the average number of outages this has caused the site in the last 5 years.

Standard 5. Maintain mitigation options and plans to eliminate or reduce the potential impact to a mission in the event of a natural gas supply disruption with the appropriate government and commercial natural gas distributors and onsite owners/operators (e.g., storage facilities, looped distribution systems, and secondary service meters, etc.) and identify the network's SPFs if applicable.

Benchmark 5.1. Review natural gas supply-related contingency plans to answer the following:

Question 5.1.1. Does the site maintain a contingency plan to ensure the availability of natural gas supplies to accomplish its mission? YES / NO

If NO, skip to Benchmark 6.1.

If YES, request a copy.

Question 5.1.2. Does this plan enlist external parties (e.g., DESC POC or natural gas providers, etc.)? YES / NO

If NO, skip to Question 5.1.5.

Question 5.1.3. Has this plan been coordinated and signed by external parties? YES / NO

Question 5.1.4. Have there been any difficulties in getting these units when needed? YES / NO

If YES, explain.

Question 5.1.5. Does the site maintain contingency plans to ensure immediate repairs or workarounds of the natural gas system to ensure support to the community? YES / NO

Question 5.1.6. Are the necessary personnel required to implement these plans available to respond onsite at all times? YES / NO

Question 5.1.7. Are emergency drills performed to test the site's ability to alternately route natural gas supplies to the community? YES / NO

Question 5.1.8. Has the plan been protected and not released to the public? YES / NO

Question 5.1.9. What date was the plan last reviewed and updated?

Question 5.1.10. What date was the plan last exercised?

Standard 6. Conduct routine preventive maintenance and testing of natural gas system components to ensure that the system remains in a reliable and safe condition to preclude operational failure, resulting from natural degradation (e.g., spare parts, maintenance personnel, etc.).

Benchmark 6.1. Determine if the routine preventive maintenance and testing of natural gas system components at the site is sufficient for normal operation. NOTE: Repeat for each region, community or business sector that relies on natural gas.

Question 6.1.1. Does the site perform routine preventive and corrective maintenance of the natural gas system? YES / NO

Question 6.1.2. Does the site maintain logs or files that document the age and maintenance history of the natural gas system and components? YES / NO

Question 6.1.3. Are periodic surge and/or emergency operations and end-to-end drills conducted to test the natural gas distribution's primary and/or backup systems under full-demand conditions? YES / NO

Question 6.1.4. Identify the organization that conducts the testing and exercises.

Question 6.1.5. How often are tests and exercises conducted (number of tests each year)?

Question 6.1.6. Are the results of tests and exercises documented for future trend reviews? YES / NO

Question 6.1.7. Have any natural gas system components malfunctioned or failed to operate in the past? YES / NO

If YES, describe the occurrence.

Question 6.1.8. What corrective actions were taken to resolve the issues in Question 6.1.7?

Question 6.1.9. Are the trained maintenance, technical, and operations staffs available to operate and maintain the natural gas system during normal, backup, emergency, and no electric power scenarios? YES / NO

Question 6.1.10. Are there documented procedures for surge/emergency operations of the natural gas system and system recovery? YES / NO

Benchmark 6.2. Determine if the site maintains sufficient component inventories, part replacement contingencies, maintenance personnel, expertise, and contingency plans to guarantee mission accomplishment? (Repeat for each region, community or business sector that relies on natural gas.)

Question 6.2.1. Does the site conduct natural gas system component inventories? YES / NO?

Question 6.2.2. Are sufficient spare parts and consumables available to meet the endurance limitations of backup systems to correct casualties to primary natural gas systems supporting critical missions? YES / NO

Question 6.2.3. Does the site have local alternative sources for spare parts and consumables? YES / NO

Benchmark 6.3. Describe operational procedures for the site by answering the following: (Repeat for each region, community or business sector that relies on natural gas.)

Question 6.3.1. Are all site operators and maintainers available to respond onsite at all times? YES / NO

Question 6.3.2. Identify those skill sets or positions where only one individual is capable of performing operational or maintenance duties. (None or identify position or skills.)

Standard 7. Identify dependencies on and support provided to other SFINs.

Benchmark 7.1. Identify the site's SFIN interdependencies by answering the following:

Question 7.1.1. Does the natural gas system require electricity to operate? YES / NO

If YES, provide the reason.

Question 7.1.2. Does the natural gas system require petroleum to operate? YES / NO

If YES, provide the reason.

Question 7.1.3. Does the natural gas system require road transportation to operate? YES / NO

If YES, provide the reason.

Question 7.1.4. Does the natural gas system require rail transportation to operate? YES / NO

If YES, provide the reason

Question 7.1.5. Does the natural gas system require air transportation to operate? YES / NO

If YES, provide the reason.

Question 7.1.6. Does the natural gas system require water transportation to operate? YES / NO

If YES, provide the reason.

Question 7.1.7. Does the natural gas system require any communications systems to operate? YES / NO

If YES, provide the reason.

Question 7.1.8. Does the natural gas system require potable water to operate? YES / NO

If YES, provide the reason.

Question 7.1.9. Does the natural gas system require wastewater to operate? YES / NO

If YES, provide the reason.

Question 7.1.10. Does the natural gas system require chemicals to operate? YES / NO

If YES, provide the reason.

Question 7.1.11. Does the natural gas system require HVAC to operate? YES / NO

If YES, provide the reason.

STOP: If you answered YES for any of Questions 7.1.1 through 7.1.11, ensure that you accomplish the benchmark for that area.

A.3. Energy - Petroleum.

Petroleum is broad term that includes all crude and refined petroleum products, but for the purpose of these assessment standards "petroleum" refers solely to refined petroleum products, such as jet fuel, marine fuels, diesel, gasoline and lubricants used directly or indirectly by the affected region, community, or business sector. Refined petroleum infrastructure networks consist primarily of refineries, refined products pipeline systems, valve pits, storage tank farms, distribution terminals (load racks), pump stations, fueling and defueling stations, tanker berths, mooring systems, quality assurance labs, and hydrant fueling systems. The petroleum infrastructure is highly dependent on the transportation infrastructure to ship products to intermediate or end users via maritime, road, air, and rail. The primary goal of assessing the petroleum network is to determine if the supply network at a given location and the supporting offsite petroleum power system have the capacity, redundancy, path diversity, security, survivability, and reliability to properly support a region, community, or business sector.

- STANDARD 1. Maintain documents detailing the current configuration of the petroleum system that directly supports the region, community or business sectors (e.g., drawings, maps, blueprints, and schematics).

- STANDARD 2. Determine if the petroleum system has the ability to meet current and identified future petroleum needs of the region, community or business sector (e.g., capacity, redundancy, path diversity, and reliability, etc.).

- STANDARD 3. Identify all system assets essential to supporting the continued and reliable delivery of petroleum.

- STANDARD 4. Maintain security to protect against threats/hazards commensurate with the needs and resources of all identified critical petroleum assets. DOD Components may work with the commercial or municipal entities owning petroleum products delivery equipment and installations to enhance equipment security on a case-by-case basis.

- STANDARD 5. Maintain mitigation options and plans to eliminate or reduce the potential impact to a mission in the event of a petroleum supply disruption with the appropriate petroleum distributors and onsite owner/operators (e.g., alternative source terminals, portable storage, etc.) and identify the system's single points of failure (SPFs) if applicable.

- STANDARD 6. Conduct routine preventive maintenance and testing of petroleum system components to ensure that the system remains in a reliable and safe condition to preclude operational failure, resulting from natural degradation (e.g., spare parts, maintenance personnel, etc.).

- STANDARD 7. Identify dependencies on and support provided to other SFINs.

Applicability Test:

(1) Does the site use petroleum products? YES / NO

(2) Will the lack of these petroleum products prevent or negatively impact mission timelines or full-mission accomplishment? YES / NO

Standard 1. Maintain documents detailing the current configuration of the petroleum system that directly supports the DCAs (e.g., drawings, maps, blueprints, and schematics).

Benchmark 1.1. Review site petroleum drawings, maps, blueprints, and schematics to answer the following:

Question 1.1.1. Are maps, drawings, schematics, or blueprints maintained and available that show network component locations, connections, operational & design parameters, access points, and network control systems, etc. (ArcMap shape files, Computer Aided Design (CAD) drawings, and Geographical Information System (GIS) are the preferred formats)? YES / NO

If YES, request copies in the preferred formats.

If NO, skip to Benchmark 2.1.

Question 1.1.2. Are the major petroleum system components identified in the drawings (e.g., compressors, pumps, storage facilities, and receipt or delivery points)? YES / NO

If YES, identify each component.

Question 1.1.3. Are the documents current as of the date of the assessment? YES / NO

If NO, when were they last updated?

Question 1.1.4. Has this information been protected, not been made available to the public, and kept in a secure onsite location? YES / NO

Question 1.1.5. Are any of the maps necessary for mission completion? YES / NO

If YES, answer Question 1.1.6.

Question 1.1.6. Are there duplicate copies of these documents or drawings backed up offsite? YES / NO

STOP: Collect/submit any electronic copies of these documents with your final data for database review.

Standard 2. Determine if the petroleum system has the ability to meet current and identified future petroleum needs of DCAs (e.g., capacity, redundancy, path diversity, and reliability, etc.).

Benchmark 2.1. Identify the petroleum requirements for the mission element or function.

Question 2.1.1. List the consumption and storage (days of supply) requirements (by type).

Benchmark 2.2. Identify petroleum distributors' relationship to the site by answering the following:

Question 2.2.1. What types of petroleum products and their quantities are available at the site?

Question 2.2.2. Who are the petroleum distributors serving the site? Identify company name, company address, and types of fuel provided.

Question 2.2.3. Who are the petroleum distributors' points of contact (POCs)? Identify POC by office symbol, office name, and telephone numbers.

Question 2.2.4. What are the site's contracted quantities of petroleum by the petroleum distributor? Identify by name and contracted quantity for distribution, volume, type of product, frequency of delivery, and contract timeframes.

Question 2.2.5. How is the petroleum delivered to the site (e.g., pipeline, tanker, barge, tanker truck, or railcar)?

Question 2.2.6. What is the petroleum distributors' priority of petroleum service to this site compared with other petroleum customers? Identify by name or type those customers the petroleum distributors place ahead of the site (e.g., hospitals or residential customers, etc.).

Benchmark 2.3. Relationship with Defense Energy Support Center (DESC) (Deleted)

Benchmark 2.4. Describe the site's petroleum infrastructure owner to the site by answering the following:

Question 2.4.1. Identify the petroleum infrastructure owner at the site (e.g., company name, company address, and telephone numbers).

Question 2.4.2. Who are the owner's POCs? Identify POC by office symbol, office name, and telephone numbers.

Question 2.4.3. Does the site have an emergency provisions contract with fuel providers? YES / NO

Question 2.4.4. Does the site receive priority restoration of fuel deliveries? YES / NO

If YES, describe.

Question 2.4.5. Does the owner subcontract any services (e.g., maintenance or lab services)? YES / NO

If YES, identify POC by office symbol, office name, and telephone numbers.

Benchmark 2.5. Describe the site's petroleum infrastructure operator of the site by answering the following: (If the owner is the operator, skip to Benchmark 2.6.)

Question 2.5.1. Identify the petroleum system operator of the site (e.g., company name, company address, and telephone numbers).

Question 2.5.2. Who are the operator's POCs? Identify POC by office symbol, office name, and telephone numbers.

Question 2.5.3. Does the site have an emergency provisions contract with the fuel providers? YES / NO

Question 2.5.4. Does the site receive priority restoration of fuel deliveries? YES / NO

If YES, describe.

Question 2.5.5. Does the operator subcontract any services (e.g., maintenance or lab services)? YES / NO

If YES, identify POC by office symbol, office name, and telephone numbers.

Benchmark 2.6. Define regional petroleum refineries that may serve the site by answering the following:

Question 2.6.1. Identify the refineries that may provide petroleum products to the site. Identify plant name, address, geolocation (i.e., decimal latitude and longitude), and total capacity (barrels per day (BPD)).

Question 2.6.2. Who are the refineries' POCs? Identify POC by office symbol, name, title, and telephone numbers.

Question 2.6.3. Identify alternate sources of petroleum processing for products used by the site. Identify plant name, address, geolocation (i.e., decimal latitude and longitude), and total capacity in BPD.

Benchmark 2.7. Define the Petroleum Distribution Terminals or Defense Fuel Support Points (DFSP) that serve the site by answering the following:

Question 2.7.1. Identify the Petroleum Distribution Terminal or DFSP that may provide petroleum products to the site. Identify terminal name, address, geolocation (i.e., decimal latitude and longitude), and total capacity in barrels.

Question 2.7.2. Who are the Petroleum Distribution Terminal or DFSP's POCs? Identify POC by office symbol, name, title/rank, and telephone numbers.

Question 2.7.3. Identify Petroleum Distribution Terminal or DFSP storage components (tanks). Identify number, type, underground or above ground, and the capacity in barrels.

Question 2.7.4. Describe products distributed by the Petroleum Distribution Terminal or DFSP (e.g., type and quantity).

Question 2.7.5. Describe Petroleum Distribution Terminal or DFSP transportation method (e.g., pipeline, barge, tanker, tank truck, railcar, capacity (BPD), and frequency of delivery).

Benchmark 2.8. Define Petroleum Distribution/Storage onsite.

Question 2.8.1. Identify primary distribution/storage components (e.g., tanks, pumping stations, storage tanks, meters, and manifolds/valve box (number, type, underground or aboveground, and capacity in barrels).

Question 2.8.2. Identify products distributed onsite (e.g., type and quantity in barrels or gallons).

Question 2.8.3. Identify alternate distribution/storage components (e.g., number, type, underground or aboveground, and capacity in barrels).

Benchmark 2.9. If the site has a petroleum monitoring and/or control systems (e.g., SCADA, etc.), answer the following; otherwise skip to Standard 3. Repeat for EACH petroleum monitoring and/or control system, if more than one supports a region, community or business sector.

Question 2.9.1. Is there a petroleum monitoring and/or control system onsite? YES / NO

If YES, identify where it is located.

If NO, skip to Standard 3. (If more than one petroleum monitoring and/or control system, identify the geolocation (i.e., decimal latitude and longitude) of each and which portions of the system they support.)

Question 2.9.2. What communications mechanism does this monitoring and/or control system use (e.g., public switched network (PSN), radio, leased lines, fiber optics, satellite, or microwave)?

Question 2.9.3. What is the age of this monitoring and/or control system?

Question 2.9.4. On what type of platform does this monitoring and/or control system operate?

Question 2.9.5. Who designed, installed, and operates this monitoring and/or control system? Identify organization, address, and contact number.

Question 2.9.6. Does the site have onsite or offsite operational and/or maintenance personnel for the monitoring and/or control system? YES / NO

If YES, list how many.

Question 2.9.7. How often are this system's operational parameters checked or monitored? Identify the number per day/week.

Question 2.9.8. Can the petroleum system supporting a critical mission or asset operate independently if this monitoring and/or control system is not operational? YES / NO

Question 2.9.9. What backup communications systems are in place for this monitoring and/or control system?

Question 2.9.10. Have operations without the monitoring and/or control system been practiced or exercised within the last 12 months? YES / NO

Question 2.9.11. Is this monitoring and/or control system protected from outside access such as an open or public communications paths (e.g., Internet, phone line, or radio frequency)? YES / NO

If YES, identify access points.

Question 2.9.12. Does the site maintain replacement components for the monitoring and/or control system or have appropriate contracts to ensure immediate response and repair? YES / NO

Standard 3. Identify all system assets essential to supporting the continued and reliable delivery of petroleum.

Benchmark 3.1. Define the key elements of site data that support critical missions and processes by answering the following:

Question 3.1.1. Identify the petroleum pipeline components that are important to the site (e.g., compressors, pumps, storage facilities, and receipt or delivery points)? Identify each type of component and its geolocation (i.e., decimal latitude and longitude).

Question 3.1.2. What types of petroleum distribution systems (e.g., pipeline, truck, etc.) are located onsite?

Question 3.1.3. What is the estimated mission-related consumption, broken down by mission requirements and types of petroleum, for average day and peak day? Identify the total estimated daily consumption of each petroleum product in gallons or barrels.

Question 3.1.4. What methods are used to test fuel quality? Provide the document number or specification.

Question 3.1.5. Where is the fuel quality tested (e.g., lab, offsite contractor office, etc.)?

Identify location by name, building number, and geolocation (i.e., decimal latitude and longitude).

Question 3.1.6. Has the site had issues with fuel quality? YES / NO

If YES, describe.

Benchmark 3.2. Identify if the site has backup petroleum products to support the missions by answering the following:

Question 3.2.1. Does the site have reserved petroleum inventory storage for each type of product identified in Question 3.1.2? YES / NO

Question 3.2.2. Is the backup storage site separate from the primary storage site? YES / NO

If YES, identify location by name, building number, and geolocation (i.e., decimal latitude and longitude), type of storage container, quantity stored by type of product, or not applicable.

Question 3.2.3. For those not stored, can another stored petroleum product onsite be substituted? YES / NO.

Identify fuel type, quantity, or not applicable.

Question 3.2.4. Based on typical usage, how long will the reserve last (number of days/hours)?

Question 3.2.5. How are these fuel reserves monitored and inventoried (describe for each fuel type; e.g., local, remote, etc.)?

Benchmark 3.3. Describe the support the site's petroleum distribution system provides to the region, community or business sector by answering the following: (Repeat for EACH system that relies on Petroleum.)

Question 3.3.1. For each identified sector, does that sector have more than one petroleum receipt point per fuel type (provide geolocation (i.e., decimal latitude and longitude) for each petroleum supply point entering the site and fuel type)?

Question 3.3.2. For each sector, what is the estimated peak consumption (identify the total estimated daily consumption of petroleum in gallons or barrels)?

Question 3.3.3. Does the sector have pre-positioned petroleum inventories? YES / NO

Question 3.3.4. Where is this inventory storage site (identify location by name, building number, and geolocation (i.e., decimal latitude and longitude), type of storage container, quantity stored, or not applicable)?

Question 3.3.5. How long will the inventory sustain business or customer-related activities (number of days or not applicable)?

Benchmark 3.4. Determine if all SPFs, based on system design components for the petroleum system supporting regions, communities and business sectors or processes, have been identified.

Question 3.4.1. Have the owner/operators of the petroleum system identified and recorded any SPF vulnerabilities of the system? YES / NO

Question 3.4.2. Identify each of these petroleum system critical components and SPFs (identify each SPF by component, cause, and geolocation (i.e., decimal latitude and longitude)).

Question 3.4.3. Is the petroleum system designed so no SPFs exist in paths linking system elements deemed critical to the operations of a network (with this design, two or more simultaneous failures or errors must occur at the same time to cause a service interruption)? YES / NO

Question 3.4.4. Where feasible, do petroleum providers, system operators, and equipment suppliers provide emergency response for supporting sector activities? YES / NO

Question 3.4.5. Have the owner/operators of the petroleum system identified remedies for the SPF vulnerabilities that may affect critical missions? YES / NO

Benchmark 3.5. Determine if all SPFs for the petroleum system's physical pathways have been identified.

Question 3.5.1. Do petroleum distribution routes have physical diversity (e.g., not co-located, not sharing rights-of-way, etc.)? YES / NO

If NO, describe.

Question 3.5.2. Where physical pathway SPFs have been identified, have resolutions been considered, such as using multiple petroleum suppliers to provide diverse connectivity to an alternate location? YES / NO

If NO, describe.

Standard 4. Maintain security to protect against threats/hazards commensurate with the needs and resources of all identified critical petroleum assets. DOD Components may need to work with the commercial or municipal entities owning petroleum product delivery equipment and installations to enhance equipment security on a case-by-case basis.

Benchmark 4.1. Determine the level of accessibility and security of the site's petroleum critical assets by answering the following:

Question 4.1.1. Are the petroleum delivery points that serve the site secured to prevent unauthorized access? YES / NO

Question 4.1.2. Identify by name and location who has access to each critical asset.

Question 4.1.3. Do all critical components of the petroleum system restrict unauthorized access from the general population, or are they buried to prevent unauthorized immediate access? YES / NO

Question 4.1.4. What portions of the petroleum system have security features (e.g., video surveillance, intrusion-detection systems, fire suppression, etc.)? Describe security measures.

Question 4.1.5. Do site security agents regularly check the security of external portions of the petroleum system to detect attempts of unauthorized access? YES / NO

Question 4.1.6. Are all SPFs and critical elements of the site's petroleum system protected by access-control measures to prevent unauthorized access? YES / NO

Question 4.1.7. Would any attempt to interrupt or contaminate the petroleum flow be detected by the site? YES / NO

Benchmark 4.2. Determine the susceptibility level of the site's petroleum system to chemical, biological, radiological, nuclear, explosive (CBRNE) events. (Deleted)

Benchmark 4.3. Determine the susceptibility level of the site's petroleum system to explosion/sabotage or projectile impact effects.

Question 4.3.1. Does the site have the capability to detect explosive threats in delivery vehicles or mail delivery? YES / NO.

If Yes, what are the threshold detection levels?

Question 4.3.2. Does the site have dedicated Explosive Ordnance Disposal (EOD) support? YES / NO

Question 4.3.3. Do EOD personnel have training or contingency plans for dealing with threats near petroleum system elements? YES / NO

Question 4.3.4. Are petroleum system operators and maintenance personnel trained in procedures of what to do if they find suspicious packages near petroleum system elements? YES / NO

Question 4.3.5. Have EOD and petroleum systems operators and maintenance personnel practiced or exercised operations in EOD removal near petroleum systems within the past 12 months? YES / NO

Question 4.3.6. Identify those locations and key elements of the site's petroleum system (e.g., apartments, offices, or roads, etc.) that are observable to offsite locations (provide geolocation (i.e., decimal latitude and longitude) and describe general degree window of observation.).

Question 4.3.7. Does hunting take place within 1 mile of the site? YES / NO

Benchmark 4.4. Determine the susceptibility level of the site's petroleum system to cyber threats. (Repeat for all germane components.)

Question 4.4.1. Which elements of the petroleum system are electronically accessible to the outside world (provide component name, identification, and describe accessibility (telephone line or modem, etc.)?

Question 4.4.2. Have those key petroleum systems with computer automation been subjected to a cyber threat evaluation? YES / NO. Describe the evaluation.

Question 4.4.3. What were the identified vulnerabilities to automated petroleum system components by this inspection?

Question 4.4.4. Are systems protected against electromagnetic interference (EMI)? YES / NO

Question 4.4.5. Are systems protected against radio frequency interference (RFI)? YES / NO

Question 4.4.6. Are systems protected against energy-particle disruption? YES / NO

Question 4.4.7. Are systems protected against signal jamming? YES / NO

Question 4.4.8. Is information important to security protected from the public to include encryption of stored data? YES / NO

Question 4.4.9. Is information important to security protected from the public to include encryption of communications? YES / NO

Question 4.4.10. Identify and describe the corrective measures and quantitatively report the estimated reduction in vulnerability that has been put into place to mitigate these cyber vulnerabilities.

STOP: The DCIP community highly recommends that all sites have an independent cyber inspection of those systems that support critical missions no less frequently than every three years to evaluate these systems against current threats.

Benchmark 4.5. Determine the susceptibility level of the site to arson.

Question 4.5.1. Are any components of the petroleum system an attractive target for or uniquely susceptible to arson (large stores of combustibles, etc.)? YES / NO

Question 4.5.2. Identify the locations that are attractive or susceptible to arson.

Benchmark 4.6. Determine the historical level of the site's petroleum system to intentional or accidental man-made damage mechanism events.

Question 4.6.1. Has the site ever experienced petroleum system outages? YES / NO

If YES, describe what caused the outages, how often the outages occurred, and what were the durations of the outages?

Question 4.6.2. Identify the average number of outages (and source of the outage) this has caused the site in the last five years.

Benchmark 4.7. Determine the susceptibility of the site's petroleum system elements that support regions, communities and business sectors to natural disasters (earthquakes, hurricanes, fire, and weather effects heat, cold, wind, etc.). Repeat for all qualifying components.

Question 4.7.1. Identify those key petroleum system components susceptible to damaging wind effects up to normal area maximums (provide component name, identification, wind speed, and/or duration limitations).

Question 4.7.2. Identify the key petroleum system components susceptible to blowing debris (provide component name, identification, wind speed, and/or duration limitations).

Question 4.7.3. Are trees or other standing objects located far enough from petroleum system components that, if they fell, they would not impact the petroleum system? YES / NO

Question 4.7.4. Based on Questions 4.7.1 through 4.7.3, what is the lowest wind speed at which mission-impacting damage begins to occur to the petroleum system components (provide component name, identification, and wind speed)?

Question 4.7.5. Are key petroleum system components protected from electrical surge or lightning strike? YES / NO

Question 4.7.6. Which petroleum system components are vulnerable to damage from electrical surge and/or lightning effects, and at what level of voltage will this damage occur (provide component name, identification, and voltage level)?

Question 4.7.7. Are key petroleum system components protected from rain, water, and flooding effects? YES / NO

Question 4.7.8. Which petroleum system components are vulnerable to water damage (provide component name, identification, and describe the reason)?

Question 4.7.9. Describe the rain, water, and flooding conditions that would cause damage to petroleum system components (e.g., flash flooding, the approximate flooding depth at which damage would occur, etc.).

Question 4.7.10. Are key petroleum system components protected from environmental heat and humidity (i.e., not fire) effects? YES / NO

Question 4.7.11. Which petroleum system components are vulnerable to heat damage (provide component name, identification, and describe the reason)?

Question 4.7.12. Describe the tolerances of the petroleum system components to heat and humidity (not fire) effects (e.g., temperature and humidity levels at which operations are disrupted or fail).

Question 4.7.13. Are key petroleum system components resistant to cold and icing effects? YES / NO

Question 4.7.14. Which petroleum system components are vulnerable to cold icing damage (provide component name, identification, and describe the reason)?

Question 4.7.15. Describe the tolerances of the petroleum system components to cold and icing effects (e.g., temperature or weight of ice at which asset fails or operations are disrupted).

Question 4.7.16. Are key petroleum system components protected from hail damage? YES / NO

Question 4.7.17. Which petroleum system components are vulnerable to hail damage (provide component name, identification, and describe the reason)?

Question 4.7.18. Describe the hail size that would cause critical damage to petroleum system components (e.g., any hail, ¾ to 1, 1 to 1½, or larger than 1½ inch, etc.).

Question 4.7.19. Are key petroleum system components resistant to snow accumulation? YES / NO

Question 4.7.20. Which petroleum system components are vulnerable to snow accumulation (provide component name, identification, and describe the reason)?

Question 4.7.21. Describe the tolerances of the petroleum system components to snow accumulation (e.g., feet of snow accumulation in a 24-hour period that would cause operations to be disrupted or fail).

Question 4.7.22. Is the site located outside areas where unique events such as tsunamis, earthquakes, mudslides, forest fires, or dam failures may occur? YES / NO

If YES, skip to Question 4.7.25.

Question 4.7.23. Describe which unique condition per Q 4.7.22 the site is located near.

Question 4.7.24. Does the site maintain contingency plans that address any possible unique event to that location? YES / NO

Question 4.7.25. Does the site maintain a capability of informing personnel and organizations of potentially dangerous weather conditions? YES / NO

If YES, using what methods? How quickly? Time to inform?

Question 4.7.26. Are petroleum system operators and maintenance personnel trained in procedures for operating during dangerous weather conditions? YES / NO

Question 4.7.27. Have petroleum system operators and maintenance personnel practiced or exercised operations in performing duties during dangerous weather within the past 12 months? YES / NO

Benchmark 4.8. Determine the susceptibility level of the site's petroleum system to fire.

Question 4.8.1. Does a certified Fire Inspector inspect the site's petroleum system, at least annually? YES / NO

Question 4.8.2. Are the identified hazards of fire inspections regularly tracked until all corrective actions have been taken? YES / NO

Question 4.8.3. Are fire-suppression systems available by all components of the petroleum system? YES / NO.

If Yes, how long does it take to access fire-suppression systems?

Question 4.8.4. Are emergency breathing devices available to assist petroleum system personnel in fire suppression or evacuation? YES / NO

If Yes, how many devices are needed? How many are on hand?

Question 4.8.5. Does an emergency lighting capability exist to assist petroleum system personnel in fire suppression or evacuation? YES / NO

Is the level of lighting adequate? YES / NO

Question 4.8.6. Are all petroleum system operators and maintenance personnel trained in fire-response activities? YES / NO

Question 4.8.7. Are responding fire-fighter personnel trained and equipped for dealing with petroleum system fires? YES / NO

Question 4.8.8. Can the petroleum system supply be continued regardless of where a fire may occur? YES / NO

If YES, proceed to Question 4.8.10.

Question 4.8.9. Which elements of the petroleum system, if on fire, would cause a disruption to the petroleum system (provide component name, identification, geolocation (i.e., decimal latitude and longitude), and level of interruption (full or partial)?

Question 4.8.10. Have petroleum system operators, maintenance, and fire-response personnel practiced or exercised fire response on the petroleum system within the past 12 months? YES / NO

Benchmark 4.9. Determine the susceptibility level of the site's petroleum system to other natural/accidental threats.

Question 4.9.1. Is all construction and digging onsite coordinated through a single office and capable of comparing the location to that of petroleum system elements? YES / NO

Question 4.9.2. Is the site's petroleum system susceptible to mission failure due to work stoppage or strike? YES / NO.

Identify appropriate groups or unions.

Question 4.9.3. Is the site's petroleum system susceptible to mission failure due to animal activity? YES / NO.

Identify the susceptibility.

Benchmark 4.10. Determine the historical level of the site's petroleum system to natural disaster events.

Question 4.10.1. Has the site ever experienced petroleum system outages? YES / NO

If YES, describe what caused the outages, how often the outages occur, and what were the durations of the outages?

Question 4.10.2. Identify the average number of outages this has caused the site in the last five years.

Standard 5. Maintain mitigation options and plans to eliminate or reduce the potential impact to a mission in the event of a petroleum supply disruption with the appropriate petroleum distributors and onsite owner/operators (e.g., alternative source terminals, portable storage, etc.) and identify the system's single points of failure (SPFs) if applicable.

Benchmark 5.1. Review petroleum supply-related contingency plans to answer the following:

Question 5.1.1. Does the site maintain a contingency plan to ensure the availability of petroleum supplies to accomplish its mission? YES / NO

If NO, skip to Benchmark 6.1.

If YES, request a copy.

Question 5.1.2. Does this plan enlist external parties (e.g., DESC POC or petroleum providers, etc.)? YES / NO

If NO, skip to Question 5.1.5.

Question 5.1.3. Has this plan been coordinated and signed by external parties? YES / NO

Question 5.1.4. Have there been any difficulties in getting these units when needed? YES / NO

If YES, explain.

Question 5.1.5. Does the site maintain a contingency plans to ensure immediate repairs or workarounds to the petroleum system to ensure support to the region, community or business sector? YES / NO

Question 5.1.6. Are the necessary personnel required to implement these plans available to respond onsite at all times? YES / NO

Question 5.1.7. Are emergency drills performed to test the site's ability to alternately route petroleum supplies? YES / NO

Question 5.1.8. Has the plan been protected and not released to the public? YES / NO

Question 5.1.9. What date was the plan last reviewed and updated?

Question 5.1.10. What date was the plan last exercised?

Standard 6. Conduct routine preventive maintenance and testing of petroleum system components to ensure that the system remains in a reliable and safe condition to preclude operational failure, resulting from natural degradation. (e.g., spare parts, maintenance personnel, etc.).

Benchmark 6.1. Determine if the routine preventive maintenance and testing of petroleum system components at the site is sufficient for continued customer service (Repeat for each service that relies on Petroleum.)

Question 6.1.1. Does the site perform routine preventive and corrective maintenance of the petroleum system? YES / NO

Question 6.1.2. Does the site maintain logs or files that document the age and maintenance history of the petroleum system and components? YES / NO

Question 6.1.3. Are periodic surge/emergency operations and end-to-end drills conducted to test the petroleum distribution's primary and/or backup systems under full-demand conditions? YES / NO

Question 6.1.4. Identify by organization who conducts the testing and exercises.

Question 6.1.5. How often are the tests and exercises conducted? Identify the number of tests conducted each year.

Question 6.1.6. Are the results of the tests and exercises documented for future trend reviews? YES / NO

Question 6.1.7. Have any petroleum system components malfunctioned or failed to operate in the past? YES / NO.

If YES, describe the occurrence.

Question 6.1.8. Identify and describe the corrective actions that were taken to resolve the issues in Question 6.1.7.

Question 6.1.9. Are the trained maintenance, technical, and operations staffs available to operate and maintain the petroleum system during normal, backup, emergency, and no electric power scenarios? YES / NO

Question 6.1.10. Are there documented procedures for surge/emergency operations of the petroleum system and system recovery? YES / NO

Benchmark 6.2. Determine if the site maintains sufficient component inventories, part replacement contingencies, maintenance personnel, expertise, and contingency plans to guarantee continuing operations. (Repeat for each sector that relies on Petroleum.)

Question 6.2.1. Does the site conduct petroleum system component inventories? YES / NO

Question 6.2.2. Are sufficient spare parts and consumables available to meet the endurance limitations of backup systems to correct casualties to primary petroleum systems supporting critical missions? YES / NO

Question 6.2.3. Does the site have local alternative sources for spare parts and consumables? YES / NO

Benchmark 6.3. Describe the operational procedures for the site by answering the following: (Repeat for each sector that relies on Petroleum.)

Question 6.3.1. Are all site operators and maintainers available to respond onsite at all times? YES / NO

Question 6.3.2. Identify those skill sets or positions where only one individual is capable of performing operational or maintenance duties. (None or identify position or skills)

Question 6.3.3. Does the site practice safe operating procedures at all times; e.g., grounding and bonding? YES / NO

Standard 7. Identify dependencies on and support provided to other SFINs.

Benchmark 7.1. Identify the site's SFIN interdependencies by answering the following:

Question 7.1.1. Does the petroleum system require electricity to operate? YES / NO

If YES, describe and provide the reason.

Question 7.1.2. Does the petroleum system require natural gas to operate? YES / NO

If YES, describe and provide the reason.

Question 7.1.3. Does the petroleum system require road transportation to operate? YES / NO.

If YES, describe and provide the reason.

Question 7.1.4. Does the petroleum system require rail transportation to operate? YES / NO.

If YES, describe and provide the reason.

Question 7.1.5. Does the petroleum system require air transportation to operate? YES / NO.

If YES, describe and provide the reason.

Question 7.1.6. Does the petroleum system require water transportation to operate? YES / NO.

If YES, describe and provide the reason.

Question 7.1.7. Does the petroleum system require any communications systems to operate? YES / NO.

If YES, describe and provide the reason.

Question 7.1.8. Does the petroleum system require potable water to operate? YES / NO

If YES, describe and provide the reason.

Question 7.1.9. Does the petroleum system require wastewater to operate? YES / NO

If YES, describe and provide the reason.

Question 7.1.10. Does the petroleum system require chemicals to operate? YES / NO

If YES, describe and provide the reason.

Question 7.1.11. Does the petroleum system require HVAC to operate? YES / NO

If YES, describe and provide the reason.

STOP: If you answered YES for any of Questions 7.1.1 through 7.1.11, ensure that you accomplish the benchmark for that area.

(N/A) Chemicals and Chemical Products - Chemical Storage and Use (N/A)

A.4. Water Systems - Potable, Industrial, Fire Fighting, and Wastewater.

Water systems are the means by which water is extracted, treated, stored, and delivered to consumers. Installation or facility water systems comprise supply, distribution, pumping, treatment, filtering, storage, and reserve components.

- STANDARD 1. Maintain documents detailing the current configuration of the water systems that directly support the region, community or business sector (e.g., drawings, maps, blueprints, and schematics).

- STANDARD 2. Determine if the water systems have the ability to meet current and identified future water needs (e.g., capacity, redundancy, and reliability, etc.).

- STANDARD 3. Identify all system assets essential to supporting continued and reliable delivery of water..

- STANDARD 4. Maintain security to protect against threats and/or hazards commensurate with the needs and resources of all identified critical water systems assets. Department of Defense (DOD) Components may need to work with the commercial or municipal entities owning water systems equipment and installations to enhance equipment security on a case-by-case basis.

- STANDARD 5. Maintain mitigation options and plans to eliminate or reduce the potential impact to customers in the event of significant degradation or failure of an essential water system asset (e.g., storage tanks, pumps, etc.)

- STANDARD 6. Conduct routine preventive maintenance and testing of water system components to ensure that the system remains in a reliable and safe condition to preclude operational failure, resulting from natural degradation (e.g., spare parts, maintenance personnel, etc.).

- STANDARD 7. Identify dependencies on and support provided to other SFINs.

Standard 1. Maintain documents detailing the current configuration of the water systems that directly support the region, community or business sector (e.g., drawings, maps, blueprints, and schematics).

Benchmark 1.1. Collect all documentation detailing the general system that supports all customers.

Question 1.1.1. Does the site maintain current drawings, blueprints, maps, schematics, timetables, line drawings, and photographs of potable water system key assets? YES / NO

If NO, skip to Standard 2.

1.1.1.1. Are Geographical Information System (GIS) or Computer-aided Design (CAD) formats available?

Question 1.1.2. Do these products identify the water system's key components that are important to the installation or mission (e.g., treatment plants, wells, and pumping stations, etc.), and where are they located?

Question 1.1.3. What date was the last revision of the items identified in Question 1.1.1?

Question 1.1.4. Has this information been protected, not been made available to the public, and kept in a secure onsite location? YES / NO

Question 1.1.5. Are duplicate copies of these documents or drawings backed up offsite? YES / NO

Standard 2. Determine if the water systems have the ability to meet current and identified future water needs (e.g., capacity, redundancy, and reliability, etc.).

Benchmark 2.1. Define the water distribution provider to the site.

Question 2.1.1. Who is the onsite and offsite water distribution provider (e.g., provider's name and address)?

Question 2.1.2. Who are the water distribution provider's points of contact (POCs) (e.g., POCs office symbol, office name, and telephone number)?

Question 2.1.3. What type of contract does the site have with the water distribution provider?

Question 2.1.4. Does the site have an emergency provisions contract with the water provider (e.g., describe and provide copy)? YES / NO

Benchmark 2.2. Define the water distribution operator/maintainer to the site (If the operator/ maintainer is the same as the provider, list in remarks and proceed to Benchmark 2.3.)

Question 2.2.1. Who is the onsite and/or offsite water distribution operator/maintainer (e.g., operator/maintainer's name and address)?

Question 2.2.2. Who are the water distribution operator and/or maintainer's POCs (e.g., POCs by office symbol, office name, and telephone number)?

Question 2.2.3. What type of contract does the site have with the service provider?

Question 2.2.4. Does the site have an emergency provisions contract with the provider (e.g., describe and provide copy)?

Benchmark 2.3. Identify and determine if the site's water distribution system is properly designed to ensure critical mission accomplishment.

Question 2.3.1. Who is the primary water utility POC for the installation?
Is there a regional or local government POC for the installation? YES / NO

(Provide name and contact numbers for each as applicable.)

Question 2.3.2. Where are the points of connection to the external water system and flow capacity (geolocation (e.g., decimal latitude and longitude))?

Question 2.3.3. Do external connections serve primarily as a backup to onsite water supplies? YES / NO

Question 2.3.4. What is the site's average water usage (gallons per day) (summer and winter, if significantly different)?

Question 2.3.5. How much water is required for critical mission accomplishment (gallons per day) (summer and winter, if significantly different)?

Question 2.3.6. Does the water system meet supply demands of potable, industrial, and fire-fighting water to support the critical mission? YES / NO

Question 2.3.7. Does the site's backup capability provide an adequate supply of potable, industrial, and fire-fighting water to support the critical mission? YES / NO

Question 2.3.8. How long (hours or days) will the site's storage capability sustain the demands for water during critical mission accomplishment?

Question 2.3.9. What is the operating pressure range of the network?
2.3.9.1. By areas of the system, if they are different, include system minimum and maximum pressure requirements.

Question 2.3.10. How is the water pressure maintained (describe process and backups as necessary)?

Question 2.3.11. Does the site have backup or auxiliary pumps to maintain network pressure?

Question 2.3.12. By using gravity flow, can water be distributed throughout the site?

Question 2.3.13. Is the water distribution system divided into multiple pressure zones that can be separately isolated and reconfigured to ensure an uninterrupted water supply to meet priority demands? YES / NO

Question 2.3.14. Does the site have backflow prevention devices? How many and where are they located (geolocation; i.e., decimal latitude and longitude)?

Question 2.3.15. Is there a level of automation, such as Supervisory Control and Data Acquisition (SCADA) that can detect changes in the system's operation? YES / NO

Question 2.3.16. Has the site experienced disruptions to water service, or have any significant events occurred in the past that affected water service? YES / NO

How often do they occur? What is the average duration of the disruption? What is the impact?

2.3.16.1. Describe events of the past 5 to 10 years and the corrective actions.

Question 2.3.17. Are there sufficient onsite personnel to operate the water system during crisis or high demand, to include essential personnel designated to enter the site (e.g., natural disaster, heightened threat, or system disruption)? YES / NO

Question 2.3.18. What chemical treatments (chemical types) are used in providing water to the site, and where are they stored (provide geolocation; i.e., decimal latitude and longitude)?

Question 2.3.19. What problems have been associated with water quality? Is there a water quality report? Describe any corrective actions, if any, to prevent similar problems in the future.

2.3.19.1. Describe water quality events of the past 5-10 years and the corrective actions.

Question 2.3.20. Does the system share rights-of-ways with other infrastructures (e.g., telecommunications, road, rail, natural gas/petroleum, or other)? YES / NO

2.3.20.1. Identify the geolocation (i.e., decimal latitude and longitude) and the infrastructure that it is shared with.

Benchmark 2.4. Define the control system's design aspects for the site by answering: If the site has a water distribution Monitor and Control system (e.g., SCADA, etc.), answer the following; otherwise skip to STANDARD 3. NOTE: Repeat for EACH water distribution monitor and control system, if more than one, which supports a DCA.

Question 2.4.1. Is there a water distribution monitoring and control system (i.e. SCADA, etc.) onsite? YES / NO

If more than one water distribution monitoring and control system, identify the geolocation (i.e., decimal latitude and longitude) of each and which portions of the system, to include regions or communities, they support.

Question 2.4.2. What communications mechanism does this monitoring and control system use (e.g., public switched network (PSN), radio, leased lines, fiber optics, satellite, or microwave)?

Question 2.4.3. What is the age of this monitoring and control system?

Question 2.4.4. On what platform does this monitoring and control system operate?

Question 2.4.5. What organization (address and contact number) designed, installed, and operates this monitoring and control system?

Question 2.4.6. Does the site have onsite or offsite operational and/or maintenance personnel for the monitoring and/or control system? How many?

Question 2.4.7. How often are this system's operational parameters checked or monitored?

Question 2.4.8. What types of backup water distribution systems are in place for this monitoring and control system?

Question 2.4.9. What types of backup communications systems are in place for this monitoring and control system?

Question 2.4.10. Are water distribution system operators trained to perform required operations without the use of the monitoring and control system? YES / NO

Question 2.4.11. Have operations without this monitoring and control system been practiced or exercised within the last 12 months? YES / NO

Question 2.4.12. Is this monitoring and control system protected (i.e. passwords, access controls, etc.) from unauthorized access such as an open or public communications path (e.g., Internet, phone line, or radio frequency)? YES / NO

Question 2.4.13. Does the site maintain replacement components for this monitoring and control system, or have appropriate contracts to ensure immediate response and repair?

Standard 3. Identify all system assets essential to supporting the continued and reliable delivery of water. (Repeat for segment that relies on water.)

<u>Benchmark 3.1</u>. Define the water distribution infrastructure by answering the following:

Question 3.1.1. Trace and identify the primary water system distribution components (e.g., treatment plant, wells, tanks, pumps, distribution lines, etc.) back to its initial water source (well, river, or lake, etc.).

    3.1.1.1. Component type, water flow capacity, and geolocation (i.e., decimal latitude and longitude).

Question 3.1.2. Identify the backup water capability locations and their capacity for the site.

    3.1.2.1. Component type, water flow capacity, and geolocation (i.e., decimal latitude and longitude).

Question 3.1.3. Identify each water distribution storage location and its capacity. 3.1.3.1. Component type, water flow capacity, and geolocation (i.e., decimal latitude and longitude).

Benchmark 3.2. Ensure that the site has identified potential chokepoints, limitations, and single points of failure (SPFs) in its operations and has contingency plans in place that address these potential risks to mission assurance.

Question 3.2.1. Has a study been done to identify the SPFs and chokepoints within the onsite water system network all the way to its connection with the critical mission offsite facilities, and, if disrupted, could negatively impact operations (e.g., treatment plants, pumping stations, and storage facilities)? YES / NO

Question 3.2.2. Have the owner/operators of the water system identified and recorded any SPF vulnerabilities of the system?

Question 3.2.3. Identify all potential SPFs and chokepoints from Questions 3.2.1 and 3.2.2 along with their expected mission impact, if lost or damaged (provide geolocation (i.e., decimal latitude and longitude), type of location, and mission impact).

Question 3.2.4. Does the water system have sufficient system redundancy and separation to preclude any SPFs due to component failure, sabotage, or damage? YES / NO

Benchmark 3.3. Determine if remedies for SPFs for the water system supporting communities or processes have been identified.

Question 3.3.1. Have the owner and/or operators of the water system identified remedies for the SPF vulnerabilities that may affect critical missions? YES / NO

Describe.

Question 3.3.2. Has a workaround or a casualty mode of operation (emergency repair plan) been developed to quickly restore the water system to an operational status? YES / NO

Describe.

Question 3.3.3. Have the workarounds (e.g., casualty mode option or alternate sources of water supply) been incorporated in the site's emergency procedures and exercised within the past 12 months? YES / NO

Standard 4. Maintain security to protect against threats and/or hazards commensurate with the needs and resources of all identified critical water systems assets. Department of Defense (DOD) Components may need to work with the commercial or municipal entities owning water systems equipment and installations to enhance equipment security on a case-by-case basis.

Benchmark 4.1. Determine the level of accessibility and security of the water treatment plant supporting the site.

Question 4.1.1. Do the water treatment plant's components adhere to physical security guidelines established by the utility or established by the local jurisdiction for the given locale? YES / NO

Question 4.1.2. Are treatment plants locked and secured to prevent unauthorized access? YES / NO

Identify who monitors and responds.

Question 4.1.3. Is the treatment plant's entire perimeter secured against unauthorized access? YES / NO.

Identify who monitors and responds.

Question 4.1.4. Do treatment plants have the necessary lighting, cameras, intrusion detection systems, or alarms to provide adequate monitoring? YES / NO

Identify who monitors and responds.

Question 4.1.5. Is there backup electric power to these monitoring devices (e.g., uninterrupted power supply (UPS) or generators)? YES / NO

Question 4.1.6. Is the treatment plant staffed 24/7? YES / NO

Question 4.1.7. Is chlorine gas or other stored chemicals at the treatment plant verified at delivery and secured to prevent contamination or unauthorized access? YES / NO

Question 4.1.8. Are all water treatment plant devices (e.g., vaults, pits, and backflow prevention devices) secured to deter tampering? YES / NO

Identify who monitors and responds.

Question 4.1.9. Are all water intakes from open reservoirs equipped with biochemical sensors as part of the monitoring and control system to include shutdown? YES / NO

Describe.

Question 4.1.10. Are deliveries of chemicals and other supplies to water treatment plants made in the presence of water system personnel? YES / NO

Describe.

Benchmark 4.2. Determine the level of accessibility and security of the water conveyance and distribution components.

Question 4.2.1. Do the site's conveyance and distribution system components adhere to physical security regulations established by the site or established by the local jurisdictions for the given locale? YES / NO

Question 4.2.2. Are pump stations and wells secured? YES / NO

Identify who monitors and responds.

Question 4.2.3. Are water tanks secured? YES / NO

Identify who monitors and responds.

Question 4.2.4. Are all water intake structures secured? YES / NO

Identify who monitors and responds.

Question 4.2.5. Are all components provided with proper lighting, cameras, and alarms to enable monitoring and protection? YES / NO

Identify who monitors and responds.

Question 4.2.6. Are all vaults, pits, and backflow prevention devices secured to prevent unauthorized access or tampering? YES / NO

Identify who monitors and responds.

Question 4.2.7. Are all site water distribution system components buried or within a fence line?

Question 4.2.8. Do site security personnel regularly check the security of accessible portions of the water distribution system to detect attempts of unauthorized access? YES / NO

Question 4.2.9. Would any attempt to interrupt or contaminate the water distribution flow onsite be detected? YES / NO

Identify who monitors and responds.

Question 4.2.10. Can site security respond to all critical mission locations, chokepoints, and SPSs in a reasonable period of time to prevent interruption of water distribution? YES / NO.

Identify susceptible locations.

Question 4.2.11. Do the appropriate relationships exist between site security and outside law enforcement to protect critical mission operations?

Question 4.2.12. Are deliveries of chemicals and other supplies to conveyance and distribution components made in the presence of water system personnel? YES / NO.

Describe.

Benchmark 4.3. Determine the site's susceptibility level of the water distribution system to chemical, biological, radiological, nuclear, and explosive (CBRNE) events.(N/A)

Benchmark 4.4. Determine the site's susceptibility level of the water distribution system to explosion/sabotage or projectile impact effects.

Question 4.4.1. Does the site have capabilities to detect explosive threats in delivery/ service vehicles? YES / NO.

If YES, what are the threshold detection levels?

Question 4.4.2. Are critical water distribution assets provided with adequate standoff (25 meters) (refer to UFC)? YES / NO

Question 4.4.3. Does the site have available Explosive Ordnance Disposal (EOD) support? YES / NO

If YES, identify source, capability, and response time.

Question 4.4.4. Do EOD personnel have training or contingency plans for dealing with threats near water distribution system elements (e.g., treatment plants, chemical storage, etc.)? YES / NO

Question 4.4.5. Are water distribution system operators and maintenance personnel trained in procedures of what to do if they find 'suspicious packages' near water distribution system elements? YES / NO

Question 4.4.6. Have EOD and water distribution systems operators and maintenance personnel practiced or exercised operations in explosive identification and removal near water distribution systems within the past 12 months? YES / NO

Question 4.4.7. Identify those locations and key elements of the site's water distribution system that are observable to offsite locations (e.g., apartments, offices, roads, etc.) (geolocation (i.e., decimal latitude and longitude) and general degree window of observation).

Question 4.4.8. Does hunting take place within 1 mile of the site? YES / NO

Question 4.4.9. Does the water distribution system have measures to deter/prevent insider threats such as sabotage or contamination of the system? YES / NO

Are they scalable?

Benchmark 4.5. Determine the site's susceptibility level of the water distribution system to cyber threats. (Repeat for all qualifying components.)

Question 4.5.1. Which elements of the water distribution system are electronically accessible to the outside world (e.g., component name, identification, and accessibility (telephone line or modem, etc.))

Question 4.5.2. Have those key water distribution systems with computer automation been subjected to a cyber threat evaluation? YES / NO.

Describe the evaluation.

Question 4.5.3. Describe what the identified vulnerabilities to automated water distribution system components were by this inspection. Describe.

Question 4.5.4. Are systems protected against electromagnetic interference (EMI)? YES / NO

Question 4.5.5. Are systems protected against radio frequency interference (RFI)? YES / NO

Question 4.5.6. Are systems protected against energy-particle disruption? YES / NO

Question 4.5.7. Are systems protected against signal jamming? YES / NO

Question 4.5.8. Is information important to security protected from the public to include encryption of stored data? YES / NO

Question 4.5.9. Is information important to security protected from the public to include encryption of communications? YES / NO

Question 4.5.10. Describe what corrective measures have been put into place and quantitatively report the estimated reduction in vulnerability to mitigate these cyber vulnerabilities.

Benchmark 4.6. Determine the site's susceptibility level to arson.

Question 4.6.1. Are any components of the water distribution system an attractive target for or u*niquely susceptible to arson (large stores of combustibles, etc.)?*

Question 4.6.2. Identify these locations that are attractive or susceptible to arson (geolocation (i.e. decimal latitude and longitude) and the reason).

Benchmark 4.7. Determine the site's historical level of the water distribution system to intentional or accidental man-made damage mechanism events.

Question 4.7.1. Has the site ever experienced water distribution system outages? YES / NO

If YES, what caused the outage, how often, and what were the durations of the outages?

4.7.1.1. Identify the number of interruptions in past 5 years and each interruption's average duration time.

Question 4.7.2. Identify the average number of outages (and source of the outage) this has caused the site in the last 5 years.

Benchmark 4.8. Determine the site's susceptibility of the water distribution system elements to natural disasters (earthquakes, hurricanes, fire and also including weather effects heat, cold, and wind, etc.). (Repeat for all qualifying components).

Question 4.8.1. Identify those key water distribution system components susceptible to damaging wind effects up to normal area maximums (e.g., component name, identification, wind speed and/or duration limitations).

Question 4.8.2. Identify those key water distribution system components susceptible to blowing debris (e.g., component name, identification, wind speed and/or duration limitations).

Question 4.8.3. Are there trees or other standing objects that are located close enough to water distribution system components that, if they fell, they would impact the water distribution system? YES / NO

Question 4.8.4. Based on Questions 4.8.1 through 4.8.1, what is the lowest wind speed at which mission-impacting damage begins to occur to the water distribution system components (e.g., component name, identification, wind speed and/or duration limits)?

Question 4.8.5. Are key water distribution system components protected from electrical surge or lightning strike? YES / NO

Question 4.8.6. Which water distribution system components are vulnerable to damage from electrical surge and/or lightning effects and at what level of voltage this damage will occur (e.g., component name, identification, and voltage level)?

Question 4.8.7. Are key water distribution system components protected from rain, water, or flooding effects?

Question 4.8.8. Which water distribution system components are vulnerable to water damage (e.g., component name, identification, and reason)?

Question 4.8.9. Describe the rain, water, and flooding conditions that would cause damage to water distribution system components (e.g., flash flooding, the approximate flooding depth at which damage would occur, etc.).

Question 4.8.10. Are key water distribution system components protected from heat and humidity (not fire) effects? YES / NO

Question 4.8.11. Which water distribution system components are vulnerable to heat damage (e.g., component name, identification, and reason).

Question 4.8.12. Describe the tolerances of the water distribution system components to environmental heat and humidity (i.e., not fire) effects.

Question 4.8.13. Are key water distribution system components resistant to cold and icing effects? YES / NO

Question 4.8.14. Which water distribution system components are vulnerable to cold and icing damage (e.g., component name, identification, and reason)?

Question 4.8.15. Describe the tolerances of the water distribution system components to cold and icing effects (e.g., temperature or weight of ice at which asset fails or operations are disrupted).

Question 4.8.16. Are key water distribution system components protected from hail damage? YES / NO

Question 4.8.17. Which water distribution system components are vulnerable to hail damage (e.g., component name, identification, and reason)?

Question 4.8.18. Describe the hail size that would cause critical damage to water distribution system components (e.g., any hail, ¾-, 1-, 1 to 1.5-, or larger than 1.5-inch hail, etc.).

Question 4.8.19. Are key water distribution system components resistant to snow accumulation? YES / NO

Question 4.8.20. Which water distribution system components are vulnerable to snow accumulation (e.g., component name, identification, and reason)?

Question 4.8.21. Describe the tolerances of the water distribution system components to snow accumulation (e.g., feet of snow accumulation in a 24-hour period that would cause operations to be disrupted or fail).

Question 4.8.22. Is the site located within areas where unique events such as tsunamis, tornadoes, earthquakes, avalanches, mudslides, forest and wild fires, or dam failures, etc. may occur?

Question 4.8.23. Describe which unique condition is the site located near?

Question 4.8.24. Does the site maintain contingency plans that address any possible unique event to ensure water distribution for that location? YES / NO

Question 4.8.25. Does the site maintain a capability of informing water system personnel and organizations of potentially dangerous weather conditions? YES / NO

By what methods? How quickly?

Question 4.8.26. Are water distribution system operators and maintenance personnel trained in procedures for operating during dangerous weather conditions? YES / NO

Question 4.8.27. Have water distribution system operators and maintenance personnel practiced or exercised operations in performing duties during dangerous weather within the past 12 months? YES / NO

Benchmark 4.9. Determine the site's susceptibility level of the water distribution system to fire. NOTE: Repeat as required.

Question 4.9.1. Does a certified Fire Inspector inspect the water distribution system, at least, annually? YES / NO

Question 4.9.2. Are the identified hazards of fire inspections regularly tracked until all corrective actions have been taken? YES / NO

Question 4.9.3. Are fire-suppression systems available by all components of the water distribution system? YES / NO

How long does it take to access fire-suppression systems?

Question 4.9.4. Are emergency breathing devices available to assist water distribution system personnel in fire suppression or evacuation? YES / NO

How many devices are needed? How many are on hand?

Question 4.9.5. Does an emergency lighting capability exist to assist water distribution system personnel in fire suppression or evacuation? YES / NO

Is the level of lighting adequate?

Question 4.9.6. Are all water distribution system operators and maintenance personnel trained in fire-response activities? YES / NO

Question 4.9.7. Are responding fire-fighter personnel trained and equipped for dealing with water distribution system fires? YES / NO

Question 4.9.8. Can the water distribution system supply be continued regardless of where a fire may occur? YES / NO

If YES, proceed to Question 4.9.10.

Question 4.9.9. Which elements of the water distribution system, if on fire, would cause disruption of water distribution (e.g., component name, identification, geolocation (i.e., decimal latitude and longitude), level of interruption (full or partial)).

Question 4.9.10. Have water distribution system operators, maintenance, and fire-response personnel practiced or exercised fire response on water distribution system within the past 12 months? YES / NO

Question 4.9.11. Does the site have a dedicated fire-fighting reserve of water? YES / NO

If so, how much?

Benchmark 4.10. Determine the site's susceptibility level of the water distribution system to other natural/accidental threats.

Question 4.10.1. Is all construction and digging onsite and offsite coordinated through an organization (i.e. PWC, Miss Utility, etc.) capable of comparing location to that of water distribution system elements? YES / NO

Question 4.10.2. Is the site's water distribution system susceptible to mission failure due to work stoppage/strike? YES / NO

Identify appropriate groups/unions.

Question 4.10.3. Identify the site's susceptible water distribution system susceptible to mission failure due to animal activity.

Benchmark 4.11. Determine the site's historical level of the water distribution system to natural disaster events.

Question 4.11.1. Has the site ever experienced water distribution system outages? YES / NO

If YES, what caused the outage, how often, and what were the durations of the outages?

Question 4.11.2. Identify the cause and number of interruptions and duration time this has caused the site in the last five years.

Standard 5. Maintain mitigation options and plans to eliminate or reduce the potential impact to a mission in the event of significant degradation or failure of an essential water system asset (e.g., storage tanks, pumps, etc.).

Benchmark 5.1. Identify any existing mitigation options and plans related to each identified SPF.

Question 5.1.1. Does the site/provider maintain contingency plans to ensure the availability of the potable, industrial, and fire-fighting water supply system to accomplish its mission? YES / NO

If NO, skip to STANDARD 6.

Question 5.1.2. Do these plans enlist external parties (service contractors, commercial carriers, etc.)? YES / NO

If NO, skip to Question 5.1.6.

Question 5.1.3. Have these plans been coordinated and signed/approved by the external parties? YES / NO

Question 5.1.4. Have there been any difficulties in getting these external parties when needed? YES / NO

Explain.

Question 5.1.5. Do the communications methods used by these multiple jurisdictions facilitate coordination in the event of an emergency? YES / NO

Question 5.1.6. Does the plan address the impact on water distribution operations from disruption or non-availability of water infrastructure? YES / NO

Question 5.1.7. Have the workarounds (e.g., casualty mode option, alternate modes of water supply, and reconstitution) been incorporated into the contingency and response plans? YES / NO

Question 5.1.8. Does the plan address disruption of supporting infrastructures? YES / NO

Question 5.1.9. Are the necessary personnel required to implement these plans available to respond onsite at all times? YES / NO

Question 5.1.10. Is the plan protected and not released to the public? YES / NO

Question 5.1.11. What date was the plan last reviewed and updated?

Question 5.1.12. What date was the plan last exercised?

Standard 6. Conduct routine preventive maintenance and testing of water system components to ensure that the system remains in a reliable and safe condition to preclude operational failure, resulting from natural degradation (e.g., spare parts, maintenance personnel, etc.).

Benchmark 6.1. Determine if the routine preventive maintenance, repair, and testing of water system components are sufficient.

Question 6.1.1. Does the site perform routine preventive and corrective maintenance of the water system components? YES / NO

Question 6.1.2. What high-maintenance issues or problems are recurring for the water system?

6.1.2.1. Describe (maintenance issues and/or problems and components or areas affected, frequency, duration).

Question 6.1.3. Are there any physical condition issues or problems of the water system negatively impacting its ability to function? YES / NO

6.1.3.1. Describe issues and/or problems (age, construction, material standards, etc.).

Question 6.1.4. Are periodic surge/emergency operations and end-to-end drills conducted to test the water system primary and/or alternate systems under full-demand conditions? YES/NO

Question 6.1.5. What organization conducts the testing and exercises?

Question 6.1.6. How often are the tests and exercises conducted (number of tests per year)?

Question 6.1.7. Does the site have the necessary lighting to perform water system component maintenance and repair at night? Describe (installed or mobile).

Benchmark 6.2. Determine if the spare parts inventories are sufficient for mission assurance.

Question 6.2.1. Are sufficient quantities of spare parts readily available for the water system to ensure little or no delay to mission? YES / NO

6.2.1.1. Describe part source primary and alternates (local in-house, local contract, remotely in-house, or remotely contract).

Benchmark 6.3. Define operational procedures for the site by answering:

Question 6.3.1. Are sufficient site operators and maintainers available to respond, operate, maintain, and repair the system at all times (normal and emergency)? YES / NO

Question 6.3.2. Identify those necessary skill sets or positions where less than two individuals are capable of performing these duties.

Standard 7. Identify dependencies on and support provided to other SFINs.

Benchmark 7.1. Identify the site's SFIN dependencies by answering the following:

Question 7.1.1. Does the water distribution system require electricity to operate? YES / NO

If YES, provide the reason.

Question 7.1.2. Does the water distribution system require natural gas or propane to operate? YES/NO

If YES, provide the reason.

Question 7.1.3. Does the water distribution system require petroleum to operate? YES / NO

If YES, provide the reason.

Question 7.1.4. Does the water distribution system require rail transportation to operate? YES / NO

If YES, provide the reason.

Question 7.1.5. Does the water distribution system require air transportation to operate? YES / NO

If YES, provide the reason.

Question 7.1.6. Does the water distribution system require maritime transportation to operate? YES / NO

If YES, provide the reason.

Question 7.1.7. Does the water distribution system require road transportation to operate? YES / NO

If YES, provide the reason.

Question 7.1.8. Does the water distribution system require any communications systems to operate? YES / NO

If YES, provide the reason.

Question 7.1.9. Does the water distribution system require heating, ventilating, and air conditioning (HVAC) systems to operate? YES / NO

If YES, provide the reason.

Question 7.1.10. Does the water distribution system require chemicals to operate? YES / NO

If YES, Describe and provide the reason.

A.5. Transportation- Roads and Highways

Transportation infrastructure network (Roads and Highway) refers to any land-based, non-rail network that supports a region, community or business sector of an area of responsibility. Critical networks include systems and assets within the DOD and commercial nodes.

- <u>STANDARD 1.</u> Maintain documents detailing the current configuration of the road/highway network.

- <u>STANDARD 2.</u> Determine if the road network has the ability to meet current and identified future transportation needs (e.g., capacity, redundancy, path diversity, and reliability, etc.).

- <u>STANDARD 3.</u> Identify all network assets essential to supporting the continued and reliable road operations.

- <u>STANDARD 4.</u> Maintain security to protect against threats or hazards commensurate with the needs of all critical road users.

- <u>STANDARD 5.</u> Maintain mitigation options and plans to eliminate or reduce the potential impact to a mission in the event of significant degradation or failure of an essential road asset (e.g., bridges, gates, etc.).

- <u>STANDARD 6</u>. Conduct routine preventive maintenance and road inspections to ensure that the network remains in a reliable and safe condition to preclude operational failure, resulting from natural degradation (e.g., equipment, maintenance, personnel)

Standard 1. Maintain documents detailing the current configuration of the road network that directly supports the region, community, or business sector (e.g., drawings, maps, blueprints, and schematics).

<u>Benchmark 1.1</u>. Collect all documentation detailing the general road system.

Question 1.1.1. Does the site maintain detailed maps and aerial photographs of highway transportation assets available? YES / NO

Request copies.

Question 1.1.2. Do these products identify the roadway system's key components that are important to the community (e.g., gates, etc.), and where they are located? YES / NO

<u>Benchmark 1.2</u>. Verify the documentation is accurate and that processes for maintaining documentation are in place.

Question 1.2.1. What date was the last revision of the items identified in Question 1.1.1?

Standard 2. Determine if the road network has the ability to meet current and identified future transportation needs (e.g., capacity, redundancy, path diversity, and reliability, etc.).

<u>Benchmark 2.1</u>. Describe the road infrastructure.

Question 2.1.1. Describe the road transportation network components.

Question 2.1.2. Describe the normal or designed use of onsite roads.

Question 2.1.3. What is the normal frequency of road movement onsite?

Benchmark 2.2. Describe the civil government road owners.

Question 2.2.1. Who has jurisdiction of the road system (organization, address, point of contact (POC), and phone number)?

Question 2.2.2. Who is the road maintenance provider (organization, address, POC/ position, and phone number)?

Benchmark 2.3. Describe private road owners.

Question 2.3.1. Who has jurisdiction of the private road system (organization, address, POC/position, and phone number)?

Question 2.3.2. Who is the private road maintenance provider (organization, address, POC/position, and phone number)?

Benchmark 2.4. (N/A)

Standard 3. Identify all network assets essential to providing the continued and reliable road operations.

Benchmark 3.1. Determine if the road transportation network is sufficient to meet community requirements.

Question 3.1.1. Identify the critical functions that require road assets and describe.

Question 3.1.2. Describe the critical road transportation components (chokepoints, hazardous material (HAZMAT), routes, key bridges/tunnels, and alternate routes).

Question 3.1.3. Are cargo offloading and onloading facilities capable of handling expected cargo volumes? YES / NO

Question 3.1.4. Does more than a single road access point service key community needs? YES / NO

If YES, how many and describe.

Question 3.1.5. Is the road environment free of any weight restrictions (acceptable single-axle loading 20,000 pounds) that could hamper the critical needs? YES / NO

Question 3.1.6. Identify each location onsite that has horizontal or vertical restrictions for roadway movement (type – bridge, tunnel, etc. – geolocation (i.e., decimal latitude and longitude), and restriction measurement).

Question 3.1.7. (N/A)

Question 3.1.8. (N/A)

Question 3.1.9. (N/A)

Question 3.1.10. (N/A)

Question 3.1.11. Describe road rights-of-ways shared with other infrastructures such as electric power, communications lines, etc.

Question 3.1.12. (N/A)

Question 3.1.13. What are the potential single points of failure (SPFs) and chokepoints in the road network that, if disrupted, could negatively impact the community?

   3.1.13.1. Type (loading or unloading facility, bridge, tunnel etc.);

   3.1.13.2. Geolocation (i.e., decimal latitude and longitude);

   3.1.13.3. Describe impact;

   3.1.13.4. Are alternate transportation facilities identified, and are they in the contingency plans?

Question 3.1.14. Describe any workarounds or emergency repair plans developed to restore the road system to an operational status within nominal timeline requirements.

Standard 4. Maintain security to protect against threats or hazards commensurate with the needs of all critical road users.

Benchmark 4.1. Determine the level of security of the road transportation network and key components.

Question 4.1.1. Describe controlled roadway access points, if applicable:

   4.1.1.1. Hours of operation;

   4.1.1.2. Security measures present;

   4.1.1.3. Number of lanes;

   4.1.1.4. Size or weight limitations;

   4.1.1.5. Use restrictions (e.g., trucks, HAZMAT);

   4.1.1.6. Which access point is the primary one for the community?

4.1.1.7. Describe other access points that can be used as alternatives.

Question 4.1.2. Describe security personnel that will respond to critical mission locations, chokepoints, and SPFs. What are the response times?

Question 4.1.3. (N/A)

Question 4.1.4. Have route vulnerability assessments been conducted for critical roadways supporting the joint force mission? YES / NO

Benchmark 4.2. Determine the susceptibility level of the site's road transportation network to chemical, biological, radiological, nuclear, and explosive (CBRNE) and electromagnetic pulse (EMP) events. (N/A)

Benchmark 4.3. Determine the susceptibility level of the road transportation network to explosion/sabotage or projectile impact effects.

Question 4.3.1. Do local authorities have the capability to detect explosive threats in delivery vehicles or mail delivery? YES / NO

What are the threshold detection levels?

Question 4.3.2. Is there dedicated Explosive Ordnance Disposal (EOD) support? YES / NO

Question 4.3.3. Do EOD personnel have training or contingency plans for dealing with threats near road system elements? YES / NO

Question 4.3.4. Are road system operators and maintenance personnel trained in procedures of what to do if they find "suspicious packages" near road system elements? YES / NO

Question 4.3.5. Have EOD, road systems' operators, and maintenance personnel practiced or exercised operations in EOD removal near road systems within the past 12 months? YES / NO

Question 4.3.6. Identify those key elements and locations of the site's road transportation system that are observable from offsite locations (apartments, offices, or roads etc. with their geolocation (i.e., decimal latitude and longitude) and window of observation).

Question 4.3.7. Does hunting take place within 1 mile of the site? YES / NO

Benchmark 4.4. Determine the site's susceptibility level of the road network to cyber threats. (N/A)

Benchmark 4.5. Determine the road system's susceptibility level to arson.

Question 4.5.1. Are any components of the road system an attractive target for or uniquely susceptible to arson (large stores of combustibles, etc.)? YES / NO

If YES, identify these locations that are attractive or susceptible to arson.

Benchmark 4.6. Determine the site's historical level of the road transportation network to intentional or accidental man-made damage mechanism events.

Question 4.6.1. Has the site ever experienced road network outages? YES / NO

If YES, what caused the outage, how often, and what were the durations of the outages?

Question 4.6.2. Identify the average number of outages (and source of the outage) this has caused the site in the last five years.

Benchmark 4.7. Determine the site's susceptibility of the road transportation network elements that support critical assets to natural disasters (earthquakes, hurricanes, fire, and also including weather effects heat, cold, wind, etc.).

Question 4.7.1. Identify those key road transportation network components susceptible to damaging wind effects up to normal area maximums.

Question 4.7.2. Identify those key road transportation network components susceptible to blowing debris.

Question 4.7.3. Are trees or other standing objects located far enough from road transportation network components that, if they fell, they would not impact the road transportation network? YES / NO

Question 4.7.4. Based on Questions 4.7.1 through 4.7.3, what is the lowest wind speed at which mission impacting damage begins to occur to the road transportation network components?

Question 4.7.5. Are key road transportation network components protected from electrical surge or lightning strike? YES / NO

Question 4.7.6. Which road transportation network components are vulnerable to damage from electrical surge and/or lightning effects, and at what level of voltage this damage will occur?

Question 4.7.7. Are key road transportation network components protected from rain, water, and flooding effects? YES / NO

Question 4.7.8. Which road transportation network components are vulnerable to water damage?

Question 4.7.9. Describe the rain, water, or flooding conditions that would cause damage to road system components.

Question 4.7.10. Are key road transportation network components protected from environmental heat and humidity (i.e., not fire) effects? YES / NO

Question 4.7.11. Which road transportation system components are vulnerable to heat damage?

Question 4.7.12. Describe the tolerances of the road transportation network components to heat and humidity (not fire) effects.

Question 4.7.13. Are key road transportation network components resistant to cold and icing effects? YES / NO

Question 4.7.14. Which road transportation network components are vulnerable to cold and icing damage?

Question 4.7.15. Describe the tolerances of the road transportation system components to cold and icing effects.

Question 4.7.16. Are key road transportation network components protected from hail damage?

Question 4.7.17. Which road transportation network components are vulnerable to hail damage?

Question 4.7.18. Describe the hail size that would cause critical damage to road transportation network components.

Question 4.7.19. Are key road transportation network components resistant to snow accumulation? YES / NO

Question 4.7.20. Which road transportation network components are vulnerable to snow accumulation?

Question 4.7.21. Describe the tolerances of the road transportation network components to snow accumulation.

Question 4.7.22. Is the site located outside areas where unique events such as tsunamis, earthquakes, mudslides, forest fires, or dam failures may occur? YES / NO

Question 4.7.23. Which unique condition is the site located near?

Question 4.7.24. Does the site maintain contingency plans that address any possible unique event to that location? YES / NO

Question 4.7.25. Does the site maintain a capability of informing personnel and organizations of potentially dangerous weather conditions? YES / NO

By what methods? How quickly?

Question 4.7.26. Are road transportation system operators and maintenance personnel trained in procedures for operating during dangerous weather conditions? YES / NO

Question 4.7.27. Have road transportation network operators and maintenance personnel practiced or exercised operations in performing duties during dangerous weather within the past 12 months? YES / NO

Benchmark 4.8. Determine the site's susceptibility level of the road transportation network to fire.

Question 4.8.1. Are the identified hazards of fire inspections regularly tracked until all corrective actions have been taken? YES / NO

Question 4.8.2. Are fire-suppression systems available by all components of the road transportation network? YES / NO

How long does it take to access fire-suppression systems?

Question 4.8.3. Are emergency breathing devices available to assist road transportation network personnel in fire suppression or evacuation? YES / NO

How many devices are needed? How many are available?

Question 4.8.4. Does an emergency lighting capability exist to assist road transportation network personnel in fire suppression or evacuation? YES / NO

Is the level of lighting adequate? YES / NO

Question 4.8.5. Are all road transportation network operators and maintenance personnel trained in fire-response activities? YES / NO

Question 4.8.6. Are responding fire-fighter personnel trained and equipped for dealing with road transportation network fires? YES / NO

Question 4.8.7. Can the road transportation network operations be continued regardless of where a fire may occur? YES / NO

Question 4.8.8. Which elements of the road transportation network, if on fire, would cause disruption?

Question 4.8.9. Have road system operators, maintenance, and fire-response personnel practiced or exercised fire response on the road transportation network within the past 12 months? YES / NO

Benchmark 4.9. Determine the site's susceptibility level of the road transportation network to other natural/accidental threats.

Question 4.9.1. Is all construction and digging onsite coordinated through a single office and capable of comparing location to that of road transportation network elements? YES/NO

Question 4.9.2. Is the site's road transportation network susceptible to mission failure due to work stoppage/strike? YES / NO

Question 4.9.3. Is the site's road transportation network susceptible to mission failure due to animal activity? YES / NO

Benchmark 4.10. Determine the site's historical level of the road network to natural disaster events.

Question 4.10.1. Has the site ever experienced road network outages? YES / NO

If YES, what caused the outage, how often, and what were the durations of the outages?

Question 4.10.2. Identify the average number of outages this has caused the site in the last five years.

Standard 5. Maintain mitigation options and plans to eliminate or reduce the potential impact to a mission in the event of significant degradation or failure of an essential road asset (e.g., bridges, gates, etc.).

Benchmark 5.1. Identify any existing mitigation options and plans related to each identified SPF.

Question 5.1.1. What is the contingency plan in the event that a primary road or transportation asset is not available?

Question 5.1.2. What does the contingency plan depend on (communications, external parties, etc.)?

Question 5.1.3. What is the impact if contingency plans are used (time delay)?

Question 5.1.4. What date was the plan last reviewed and updated?

Question 5.1.5. What date was the plan exercised?

Standard 6. Conduct routine preventive maintenance and road inspections to ensure that the network remains in a reliable and safe condition to preclude operational failure, resulting from natural degradation (e.g., spare parts, maintenance personnel, etc.).

Benchmark 6.1. Determine the level of preventive maintenance and testing on the road network.

Question 6.1.1. Does the site perform routine and corrective maintenance on the road transportation network? YES / NO

Question 6.1.2. How often has lack of repairs affected road operations?

Standard 7. Identify dependencies on and support provided to other SFINs.

<u>Benchmark 7.1</u>. Identify all infrastructures the road transportation network relies on to operate.

Question 7.1.1. Does the road transportation network require electricity to operate? YES / NO

If YES, provide the reason (e.g., nighttime loading operations, communications, tracking).

Question 7.1.2. Does the road transportation network require petroleum to operate? YES / NO

If YES, provide the reason (e.g., onsite fueling requirements).

Question 7.1.3. Does the road transportation network require other modes of transportation to operate? YES / NO

If YES, provide the reason (e.g., rail, air, maritime).

Question 7.1.4. Does the road transportation network require any communications systems to operate? YES / NO

If YES, provide the reason (e.g., radios).

Question 7.1.5. Does the road transportation network require chemicals to operate? YES / NO

If YES, provide the reason (e.g., salt, snow chemicals).

Intentionally Blank

APPENDIX B
SAMPLE METRICS

NOTE: *For utilities in particular, planners need to set baseline conditions and account for improvements* **operationally, financially and customer service** *and continue to periodically re survey them to document changes that have occurred since the inception of improvement programs; define ratios and other metrics that measure items of critical importance to the health and performance of the particular utility. Use these ratios to track internal improvements and to benchmark against other utilities. Some examples from various sectors follow, including significant excerpts from the MPICE.*

1. Electrical Utility

a. Finance and Accounting

(1) Debt/Equity Ratio
(2) Current Ratio
(3) Collections/Billing Ratio
(4) Billed Power/Purchased Power Ratio
(5) Days outstanding

b. Human Resources

(1) Total Staff/Total Customers
(2) Billing Staff/Total Customers
(3) Maintenance Staff/Total Customers
(4) Management/Line Staff
(5) Customer Service Staff/Total Customers

c. Customer Service

(1) Billing- Accuracy & Frequency
(2) Connections- Time to install new service & Time to restore disconnected service
(3) Repairs- Response times: customer initiated & emergency
(4) Enquiries- Response times: written & telephone

d. Quality of Service

(1) Frequency & Voltage

(a) Plus/minus range
(b) Fluctuation
(c) Imbalance
(d) Duration

  (2) Interruptions

    (a) System Average Interrupt Duration Index (SADI)
    (b) System Average Interrupt Frequency Index (SAIFI)
    (c) Customer Minutes Lost (CMI)

NOTE: *Sections 1 3 in the above indicators are common across the various utility sectors.*

2. Road Maintenance

These data are derived from the Peruvian World Bank-Inter-American Development Bank rural road maintenance program.

  a. **Transport**

    (1) Travel time
    (2) Traffic rate
    (3) Passenger fares
    (4) Freight tariffs
    (5) Road closures
    (6) Reliability of public transportation
    (7) Number of traffic accidents

  b. **Access to Services**

    (1) Number of school registered children
    (2) Number of health consultations
    (3) Number of judicial cases
    (4) Number of police interventions

  c. **Productive Activities**

    (1) Farmed land area
    (2) Land value
    (3) Productivity
    (4) Livestock ownership
    (5) Farm prices
    (6) Crop allocation
    (7) Market-oriented produce
    (8) Access to the marketplace
    (9) Access to credit
    (10) Number and income of commercial establishments
    (11) Income structure (diversification)

d. **Employment**

   (1) Type of occupation
   (2) Occupation category
   (3) Productive activity
   (4) Agricultural day's wage
   (5) Labor force structure

e. **Migration**

   (1) Number of migrants
   (2) Number of returning migrants

f. **Institutional**

   (1) Number of new institutions and/or businesses

g. **Environment**

   (1) Use of soils
   (2) Use of chemicals
   (3) Deforestation

h. **Other Travel-Related Survey Items**

   (1) Travel to farther places
   (2) Travel more frequently
   (3) Travel safely
   (4) Travel secure from assaults, violations, etc.
   (5) Obtain additional income
   (6) Access new tools or domestic artifacts
   (7) Access temporary employment
   (8) Number of infrastructure services available
   (9) % change of rural household income
   (10) Number of hours worked per week

3. Measuring Progress in a Conflict Environment

a. Delivery of Essential Government Services Strengthened

Are public expectations for provision of essential public services and utilities being met?

   • Perception of the quality of life following international intervention (By identity group).

- Level of public satisfaction with accessibility of essential government services and utilities. (By identity group)

Are the various levels of government capable of providing essential services, utilities, and functions?

- Percent of population and percent of territory receiving essential government services and utilities. (By level of government).

- Number of essential government functions being performed by international actors.

- Distribution of essential public services to identity groups relative to their percentage of the total population.

Does a professional civil service exist?

- Percentage of government employees with training and education requisite for their positions.

- Perception of the degree of corruption in the civil service. (By identity group)

- Perception of minority and majority identity groups of the degree of nepotism and /or cronyism in the civil service."[33]

The MPICE also lists quantitative outcomes, interspersed with qualitative outcomes:

h. Infrastructure Strengthened

What is the level of availability of electrical power?

- Level of public satisfaction with electrical power delivery. (By identity group and region)

- Gross electrical power output compared to pre-conflict levels.

- Extent of reliance on non-network, site-specific electrical power generation units.

- (By identity group and region)

- Prevalence, duration, and extent of brownouts and cutbacks in electrical power. (By identity group and region)

- Percentage of electricity generated from external sources

What is the level of availability of essential services?

- Percent of essential services (e.g., water, sewage, telephone, trash removal, public transportation) functioning compared with pre-conflict levels. (By identity group and region)

- Distribution of essential services to identity groups relative to their percentage of the total population.

- Level of public satisfaction with essential service delivery (By identity group and region)

- Prevalence, duration, and extent of interruptions in delivery of essential services. (By identity group and region)"[34]

Management and regulatory mechanisms are probably the most difficult to establish. Significant technical assistance is required to achieve the progress in building HN institutional capacity in these areas. The MPICE lists include a significant number of measures, including this example:

c. Fiscal Integrity Strengthened

How effective are independent oversight systems to ensure the integrity of state revenues and expenditures and to prevent diversion by predatory power structures?

- A means for the conduct of regular independent audits of state fiscal operations exists.

- Percentage of state-entity budgets/fiscal operations audited.

- Percentage of questionable financial practices investigated, prosecuted, and punished."[35]

Intentionally Blank

APPENDIX C
HEALTH SECTOR AND CONFLICT MITIGATION

1. The Dual Nature of Health Services in Stability Operations

a. The choice of where to put health sector resources (people, funding, programs) in post-conflict environments is a stability as well as a health issue. While there is evidence that a peaceful environment and good governance can contribute to the recovery of the health system, there is limited documentation on the corresponding effect of health sector programming on addressing political objectives that are central to stability operations.

b. While saving lives is an over-arching goal in the health sector, transition planning focuses on stabilizing the government and getting the country back on the development path. This requires applying health sector recourses strategically and effectively. While it is generally thought that the provision of improved health services contributes to the willingness of a population to view a new government more favorably this should not be taken as a given unless the program is planned to have an impact on specific drivers of conflict or public perceptions — for example if "power sharing" is a key mission element, then the health sector inputs must model or implement programs that bring previous combatants together in administering health resources. It is strongly advised that planners monitor the "dual objectives" to assure that there is a measureable impact on public perception, actual governance practices improved health status.

c. While health sector programming concepts have to be adapted to specific post conflict settings, there are broad lessons learned (or mistakes to avoid) from past experience in post conflict reconstruction that can guide operations. The insights throughout this section are drawn from case studies and assessments of post conflict recovery:

(1) Avoid going into going into post-conflict planning with the same mindset, program approaches, and timeframes used in development planning without adjusting them to a post-conflict transition environment that requires speed, flexibility and a mixture of immediate, short and longer term program actions.

(2) Avoid setting program priorities for health sector recovery in post conflict situations without a thorough understanding of the nature of the conflict, sufficient current information on the political and security sector as well as health assessment data and most importantly clarity on the implications and drawbacks of proposed polices and program approaches.

(3) Understand that aid resources (funding, planning and operations) in civilian organizations (USAID as well as NGOS) are often split between emergency relief/HA and development assistance. This can lead to disjointed planning which can have unintended negative consequences for the rehabilitation of national health systems. **Post-conflict transition planning needs to link short-term relief actions to a longer term "vision" or end state, if these actions are to have a positive affect on community and HN capacity.**

2. General Guidelines

"In terms of health program planning and implementation best practices in S&R environments, the following are general guidelines that probably apply across the social sectors.[36]

a. While joint USG planning is essential – in reality it is unlikely that USG resources alone will be enough to carry recovery efforts forward. Other international partners or donors, national governments and key civilian society stakeholder must be brought into the planning process.

b. Start work in advance of peace accords and invest in systems analysis of health sector and service delivery to base recovery plans on forecast of capacity restraints. Determine if actions will advance unified, non-duplicative approach. Foster close collaboration and planning between donor and the government on basic package of services, alignment of systems and interventions, commodities management and policies is critical if the government is going to be left with a coherent, county-wide system.

c. Build off of existing platforms. Not everything is destroyed during a conflict and it is useful to take a close look at institutions that survive — as these may be quite resilient and can be effective platforms to build on.

d. Balance a focus on increasing access to services with attention to the "support systems" (management information systems, finance, personnel etc) that are needed to make service delivery function.

e. In general it may be easier to motivate people around particular issues — rather than attempt a full fledged re-structuring of the sector. As a general principle offering "what people want" (i.e., curative care in a limited range of conditions) is a useful entry point to support the credibility and stability of the government.

f. Getting a limited number of services up and running rather than attempting comprehensive service provision is a reasonable approach (good enough service delivery).

g. Focus on establishing a steady supply of essential drugs and commodities and start work on building rational drug management systems. Infrastructure without a supply of drugs and commodities are of limited use.

h. Pay attention to preventive interventions. Community "demand" for prevention (immunizations; HIV/TB/malaria prevention, communicable diseases) is generally low — but may prove critical to stability. Planners need to consider what balance of curative and preventive actions are needed. While curative services may be an expressed community "need" some preventive services (i.e., disease surveillance/immunization) can't be put off to the future with out assessing the risk to destabilization. Identifying a limited number of prevention actions that are cost-effective, easily deliverable and which have a substantial impact on community livelihoods, productivity and wellbeing is a short-term planning issue that requires specialized technical assessment of both the risks and the capacity of national government structures to deliver this public service."

3. Transition Planning in the Health Sector[37]

a. The health sector is a small part of the larger post-conflict environment and a better understanding of the complex, ill-structured problems in the country is critical for making program choices about what geographic areas and targets are critical for overall mission success. Civil and military health planners need information on destabilizing factors, future events (elections), public perception of the government, equity in service provision etc. to develop realistic plans for health sector reconstruction and to determine what balance or blend of short-term service provision to longer-term re-building of public institutions that are needed to support overall mission objectives, and what is the logical sequence of actions and health sector interventions. The following broad objectives and guidance, based on past post-conflict rehabilitation can be offered.

b. **Link Relief to Transition Actions**

(1) Transition planning with the national government, other donors and NGOs on how to handle the recovery period has to start early—during the conflict or immediate relief period, to determine the architecture for future actions: conducting facility assessments and establishing decisions on reconstruction priorities; identifying human resource needs; developing policy, guidelines and standards on the essential package of services, administrative procedures, salary scale, policy etc—all the actions that will allow work to move forward rapidly post-conflict.

(2) It is important to avoid gaps in health services that will cause grievances against fragile governments. This includes important gaps that occur in going from relief activities to transitional development activities—relief actions are generally better funded than development activities and can result in fewer services as emergency actions to save lives wind down and IDP populations return to homeland.

(3) To maximize the linkage between relief and transition programs efforts should be made to: (1) build off of relief operations — using the same systems and staff from IDP camps (i.e. camp vaccinators, disease outbreak monitors); (2) Pre-positioning "umbrella" mechanisms (central contracts) with NGOs to manage small grants to make available resources for quick impact actions; Plan clusters of short-term actions with a longer-term vision or in mind;. (3) Link actions that reinforce each other and build towards more intensive longer-term development and capacity building actions. Determine what the clusters of immediate, quick impact actions that will build confidence — but will not disrupt longer- term actions such as community livelihoods, capacity building or empowerment; (4)Leave contentious measure for later phase when community capacity, confidence and credibility have grown – but start early to study the contentious issues and to sketch out interventions to assess them — look for window of opportunity and be ready with prep work so that actions can be quickly put into place (for example: fee for service); (5) Look for actions that are operationally convenient and that have potential to demonstrate what could be achieved if local government or the community adopted an approach.

c. **Manage Expectations**

(1) Technical experts (civilian or military) tend to view development activities through a technical, not a security or political lens. They look for the best technical results, not necessarily the best stability outcome. *Military planners need to be very clear that in stabilization operations that a "good enough" technical or social outcome with a high stability result is preferable to a technical success and a stability failure.*

(2) In addition to managing the technical inputs, community expectations also have to be managed. Building community confidence in a peace process or the legitimacy of a new government may be paramount, however it is equally important to distinguish between what a community may want and what can be maintained by the community itself or regional or national government. Resource requirements for the activity, the flow of military and/or donor assistance and the absorptive capacity of government to use increased funds effectively all need to be understood and part of the decision-making process if plans are to be realistic and focused on maintaining a stable environment over time.

d. **Emphasize Unity of Effort: "Basic Package of Health Services"**

(1) "Donor harmonization is the first important principle to respect in programming for the delivery of social services in post-conflict countries and it forms the basis of the OECD/DAC approach. Even though different donors may have different strategies, and even different foreign assistance objectives, it is easy to understand that all donor efforts will fail unless there is some attempt to coordinate efforts with each other and with the host government.

(2) Obviously, one difficulty in developing a harmonized approach from the donor side is the weak policy framework that is a characteristic of rebuilding states. The starting point for all donors, and for the government, should therefore be to establish a common vision of what the structure of a re-built health system would be and what services it should offer. In DR Congo, South Sudan, and Afghanistan, among others, the Basic Package of Health Services (BPHS)—prepared as a joint effort by all working or planning to work in the health sector—has proven to be an extremely valuable tool. In most instances, the BPHS specifies the physical characteristics of health facilities, their distribution on a population basis, their staffing patterns, and the specific public health interventions that will be offered at each. Health financing policies can also be included. Importantly, indicators for measuring progress toward the achievement of a stronger health system are also drafted and adopted."[38]

e. **Consider the Trade-Offs on Equity and Quality Issues**

(1) Two important considerations arise in relation to the realization of the peace dividend. The first has to do with the very important, and very desirable, attribute of equity, and is an essential feature of public health programs. However, in rebuilding states and especially in those where the prevention of renewed conflict is an important consideration, equity may not be highest priority on the agenda. Consider a situation analogous to that in South Sudan, where the only vestiges of a health system that

remained during the decades of conflict were in garrison towns and areas along the border with Khartoum-controlled Sudan. In an attempt to consolidate the peace agreement, the USG determined that these are exactly the areas at greatest risk for a renewal of hostilities and, for this reason; it is concentrating its efforts there. Health services in these areas are rudimentary at best, but are nevertheless relatively more advanced than in other, more stable areas. The best would be to work in all areas of need but the political and stability considerations dictated that—that paying less attention to the equitable distribution of health services in the short-time increases the probability of achieving and sustaining equity in the longer term.

(2) The second issue in regard to realizing a peace dividend quickly is the quality of care. Nicely built clinics stocked with medicine, but staffed with incompetent personnel, will obviously do nothing for reducing levels of morbidity and mortality in the population. Yet, developing a qualified health staff is a longer-term undertaking, inconsistent with the short-term needs of the government. This is a difficult problem to resolve, and it will require considerable attention by the government and donor community alike.[39]

f. **Address Critical Human Resource Issues**

(1) Post conflict human resources are generally limited and under-skilled; health facilities and resources are often poorly aligned to the needs of the population. In many cases the public sector simply does not have the manpower to be able to provide services. In post conflict situations Ministries of Health (MOH) may have to concentrate on the formulation of public health policies and the management (but not necessarily the implementation) of health service delivery.

(2) One approach is to make service delivery the responsibility of the private sector. For example, in Cambodia, Afghanistan, DR Congo, and South Sudan, the World Bank and other donors have championed a system of performance-based contracting between Ministries of Health and NGOs. In Afghanistan, the MOH, with initial assistance from the World Bank decided that, of the many NGOs that had been working in the country during the emergency period, one would be hired contractually to implement the BPHS in each Province. The outcome of a competitive bidding process was that one NGO, often the lead of a consortium of international and Afghanistan organizations, was given a lump-sum contract for the achievement of pre-determined performance goals. If the work was satisfactorily accomplished, the NGO received a substantial bonus. While direct contracting between the MOH and NGOs avoids creating parallel systems that have proved detrimental to the MOH the long-term impact on MOH capacity is unclear (over-reliance on using NGO partners to deliver services may draw staff away from weak government services with higher wages). The emphasis should be on formalizing accountability of NGOs to national, local government or citizens committees and to facilitate eventual integration into the public system.

(3) Other options are giving money directly to the Government — however there are often accountability issues. On the other hand, the traditional system of hiring of a contractor to oversee the issuance of grants to NGOs or to implement programs directly has been called a "state avoidance strategy" by some. Again, to a considerable

extent, staying clear of the slow and unclear decision making processes and plodding bureaucratic procedures that characterize a rebuilding MOH makes sense if speed and flexibility are the highest priority. But, in the long run, assistance to the development of efficient and effective government systems may have a longer-lasting impact by reducing the risk of a resumption of armed conflict.

APPENDIX D
REFERENCES AND ENDNOTES

PART I—REFERENCES

1. Bertini, Catherine, Executive Director; Contingency Planning Guidelines. United Nations World Food Programme, Rome, Italy (unk.).

2. Boetig, Major Brad, USAF, MC; Health Engagement Guide. White Paper, United States Joint Forces Command, Norfolk, Virginia (2008).

3. Clunan, Anne L, et al; Civil-Military Medicine: On Dangerous Ground. Naval Postgraduate School Center for Stabilization and Reconstruction Studies, Monterey, California.

4. Department of Defense Instruction 3020.45 Defense Critical Infrastructure Program (DCIP) Management, Washington, DC (April 24, 2008).

5. Dobbins, James, et al; The Beginner's Guide to Nation-Building. Rand Corporation, Santa Monica, CA (2007).

6. Dziedzic, Michael, et al; Measuring Progress in Conflict Environments (MPICE): A Metrics Framework for Assessing Conflict Transformation and Stabilization, Version 1.0. United States Institute for Peace, US Army Corps of Engineers, US Army Peacekeeping and Stabilization Institute, Washington, DC (August, 2008). Web posting at: http://handle.dtic.mil/100.2/ADA488249.

7. Field Operations Guide for Disaster Assessment and Response. Agency for International Development, Bureau for Humanitarian Response, Office of Foreign Disaster Assistance, Washington, DC (1998).

8. Greenstein, Jacob; Community Based SME for Road Maintenance. Agency for International Development, EGAT Bureau; Presentation delivered at USAID Infrastructure Workshop, Washington, DC, (December, 2007).

9. Irwin, Timothy and Chiaki Yamamoto; Some Options for Improving the Governance of State-Owned Electricity Utilities. The World Bank, Energy and Mining Sector Discussion Paper No. 11, Washington, DC (2004).

10. Lindley-French, Julian and Robert Hunter; Enhancing Stabilization and Reconstruction Operations. Center for Strategic & International Studies, Zbigniew Brzezinski Chair in Global Security And Geostrategy (CSIS). Washington, DC (2008).

11. Maxwell, Dayton, et al; Joint UK/US Civil Planning Mission to Sarajevo Final Report. Unpublished monograph dated May 1994.

12.   Morris, James T., Executive Director; Emergency Field Operations Pocketbook. United Nations World Food Programme, Rome, Italy (2002).

13.   OECD Principles of Corporate Governance. Organization for Economic Co-operation and Development, Paris, France (2004). Adobe web posting at: http://www.oecd.org/ DATAOECD/32/18/31557724.pdf.

14.   Parker, Major Kevin L., USAF; Construction in Counterinsurgency: Engineering Shifts from Support to Driving Operational Objectives. Marine Corps Gazette, June 2009. Quantico, Virginia (2009).

15.   Pavignani, Enrico; Human Resources for Health through Conflict and Recovery: Lessons from African Countries. Presentation at Sustaining Healthcare Systems in Post-Conflict Environments, US Naval Postgraduate School, Monterrey, California (2008).

16.   Ibid; Health Services Delivery in Post Conflict Fragile States. Organization for Economic Cooperation and Development, Paris, France (2005).

17.   Robinett, David et al; Held by the Visible Hand: The Challenge of SOE Corporate Governance for Emerging Markets. The World Bank, Corporate Governance, Washington, DC (2006).

18.   Schafer, Jacqueline et al; Infrastructure for Rebuilding and Developing Countries Workshop (notes and presentation slides). USAID Office of Infrastructure and Engineering, Washington, DC (2007).

19.   Schultz, Carl Gustav et al; Handbook Civil-Military Co-operation (H-CMIC). Swedish Armed Forces, Stockholm (2005).

20.   Stavridis, J., Admiral, USN; United States Southern Command- Command Strategy 2018: Partnership for the Americas. Miami, Florida (June, 2008).

21.   Sullivan, James B. and Allen Eisendrath; Operating Contracts for Managing Infrastructure Enterprises under Difficult Conditions. USAID Offices of Infrastructure and Engineering and Economic Growth & Trade, Washington, DC (2007).

22.   The Sphere Project: Humanitarian Charter and Minimum Standards in Disaster Response. The Sphere Project, Geneva, Switzerland (2004). Web postings at: http:// www.sphereproject.org.

23.   Tomb, Nicholas; Humanitarian Roles in Insecure Environments; Workshop Report. Naval Postgraduate School Center for Stabilization and Reconstruction Studies, Monterey, California (2005).

24.   Tynan, Nicola and Bill Kingdom; Optimal Size for Utilities? Returns to Scale in Water: Evidence from Benchmarking. The World Bank Group, Private Sector Development Vice Presidency, Note Number 283, (2005).

PART II—ENDNOTES

[1] Although not precisely defined, The *Interagency Assessment Framework* states, "Steady-State Engagement/Conflict Prevention Planning: May include, but is not limited to: Embassy preparation for National Defense Authorization Act (NDAA) Section 1207 funding; request by an Embassy or Combatant Command for interagency assistance in understanding and planning for leveraging US interests in fragile or at-risk countries; development of Department of Defense (DoD) Theater Security Cooperation Plans; development of Country Assistance Strategies or Mission Strategic Plans; designing interagency prevention efforts for countries listed on State Failure Watchlists and Early Warning Systems. In a steady-state or conflict prevention effort, there normally will be sufficient time and a sufficiently permissive environment to allow a full-scale assessment such as a three-day Washington, DC-based Application Workshop and several weeks of an in-country verification assessment." http://www.crs.state.gov/index.cfm?fuseaction=public.display&shortcut=CJ22.

[2] This long-established medical phrase from the Hippocratic Oath was applied to the humanitarian assistance and development world by Mary Anderson. Her book *Do No Harm: How Aid Can Support Peace Or War* (Lynne Rienner Publications, Boulder, CO (1999)) emphasizes aid's critical role as a potential lifeline to either side in a conflict, and cites examples where aid can also help societies "disengage from war."

[3] Nine major interventions have occurred during the Post-Cold War period: Iraq (twice), Somalia, Bosnia, Haiti, Rwanda, Kosovo, East Timor and Afghanistan. Panama and Granada occurred just prior to this period.

[4] This has happened frequently in past history. Liberia, Sierra Leone, and Cambodia are recent examples.

[5] Two categories of steady-state operations are countries with active strife and countries deteriorating toward crisis. Examples of the former category include Colombia, Nicaragua (in the 1970s), Nepal, Sri Lanka, Sudan, and Pakistan. Examples of the second category include the Republic of Georgia, Haiti (today), Zimbabwe, and Yemen.

[6] Examples of potable water as a top priority include providing assistance to the Kurds who had fled to the mountains in Northern Iraq following Operation DESERT STORM, to the Hutus who had fled to Goma following the Rwanda massacres in 1994, restoring the Monrovia water plant after the civil war actions in Liberia, and diverting streams to the residents of Sarajevo during the 1992-95 siege.

[7] ES&CI restoration planning and implementation actions should evolve into a steady-state process after 2-3 years. Bosnia, Afghanistan, and Iraq all required major new governance structures to transform from authoritarian systems into democratic structures and market economies.

[8] In the case of Bosnia, the establishment of a robust international force was sufficient to halt the civil war without repercussion to the intervening forces. Reconstruction funding was very limited; and reconstruction was very slow.

[9] *Guidance to the Employment of Forces*, Department of Defense, 2008.

[10] This is equally important for post-conflict reconstruction efforts, but is a pervasive requirement for Phase 0 operations.

[11] Volume One of this handbook series is: *Commander's Handbook for Participation in the Interagency Management System*. It outlines specific planning procedures and inter-relationships within the USG when an intervention is under the direction of a CRSG. It also includes extensive discussion of the *Draft USG Planning Framework*.

[12] ICAF is discussed in some detail at the S/CRS website: http://www.crs.state.gov/index.
cfm?fuseaction=public.display&shortcut=CJ22#team.

[13] Michael Dziedzic, *et al*; *Measuring Progress In Conflict Environments* (MPICE*): A Metrics Framework for Assessing Conflict Transformation and Stabilization, Version 1.0*, August, 2008, United States Institute of Peace, US Army Corps of Engineers, US Army Peacekeeping and Stabilization Institute.

[14] TRADOC Pamphlet 525-5-500, *United States Army, Commander's Appreciation and Campaign Design*, Version 1.0, January 28, 2008, p. 5.

[15] *Coalition Provisional Authority Strategic Plan*, December, 2003.

[16] *Ibid.*

[17] *Ibid.* By December, 2003 the CPA "Strategic Plan" had expanded to 150 pages of significant detail. Note that these tasks and sub-tasks are provided as real examples used in Iraq. They are not models, and were recognized, even by the activity managers at the time, as overly optimistic. This "Strategic Plan" was being created from scratch on the ground, with no precedence of strategic planning for reconstruction to draw from.

[18] Joint UK/US Civil Planning Mission to Sarajevo, Final Report, May 1994, p. 1.

[19] The United Nations High Commission for Refugees (UNHCR) defines refugees as populations that have crossed international borders, and IDPs as populations that have fled their homes but remain within their country.

[20] http://www.usaid.gov/our work/global partnerships/smart/.

[21] Stephen Bertrand, Sandro Colombo, Xavier Leus, Alessandro Loretti, *Handbook for Emergency Field Operations*, EHA/Field/99.1, World Health Organization. http://www.humanitarianinfo.org/IMToolbox/10 Reference/Handbooks Field Guides/2002 WHO Handbook For Emergency Field Operations.pdf.

[22] This section derived from notes and handouts from USAID (EGAT/I&E) workshop, Infrastructure for Rebuilding and Developing Countries, Washington, DC. December 15-19, 2008.

[23] Irwin, Timothy and Chiaki Yamamoto; <u>Some options for Improving the Governance of State-Owned Electricity Utilities</u>. World Bank Energy and Mining Sector Discussion Paper No. 11, Washington DC (2004).

[24] *Ibid.*

[25] Sullivan, James B. and Allen Eisendrath; <u>Operating Contracts for Managing Infrastructure Enterprises under Difficult Conditions</u>. USAID Offices of Infrastructure and Engineering and Economic Growth & Trade, Washington DC (2007).

[26] Dan Baum, "Mission To Sumatra: The Marines of Expeditionary Strike Group Five Take on the Tsunami," New Yorker, February 7, 2005, p. 36.

[27] Parker, Major Kevin L., USMC; <u>Construction in Counterinsurgency: Engineering Shifts from Support to Driving Operational Objectives</u>. Marine Corps Gazette, June 2009. Quantico, Virginia (2009).

[28] Ronald Inglehart an Christian Welzel, *How Development Leads to Democracy – What We Know About Modernization,* Foreign Affairs, March/April 2009, p. 39.

[29] Henriette von Kaltenborn-Stachau, *The Missing Link – Fostering Positive Citizen State Relations in Post Conflict Environments,* The World Bank, pp. 12, 14, 15. This report focuses on the relationships between the government, the media and civil society. It ominously concludes that "coordination across sectors does not take place" among donors and HN governments (p. 31).

[30] Human Development Indices: A statistical update 2008, UNDP, p. 3.

[31] *The Sphere Project. Humanitarian Charter and Minimum Standards In Disaster Response.* The Sphere Project, Geneva, Switzerland (2004).

[32] MPICE, p. 3. MPICE is oriented toward identifying the drivers of conflict and transforming the HN governance into a process that gains the confidence of the population through transparency and effectiveness.

[33] MPICE, *op cit.,* p. 16.

[34] MPICE, *op cit,* p. 43.

[35] MPICE, *op cit,* p. 43.

[36] Pavignani, Enrico; <u>Health Services Delivery in Post Conflict Fragile States</u>. Organization for Economic Cooperation and Development, Paris, France (2005).

[37] *Ibid.*

[38] Waldman, Ron; <u>Health Programming in Post-Conflict Fragile States</u>. Arlington, Virginia, USA: Basic Support for Institutionalizing Child Survival (BASICS) for the United States Agency for International Development (USAID) (2006).

[39] *Ibid.*

GLOSSARY

PART I—ABBREVIATIONS AND ACRONYMS

ACT	Advance Civilian Team
BPD	barrels per day
CACD	commander's appreciation and campaign design
CAD	computer-aided design
CBRN	chemical, biological, radiological, and nuclear
CBRNE	chemical, biological, radiological, nuclear, and high-yield explosive
CERP	Commander's Emergency Response Program
CML	customer minutes lost
CPA	Coalition Provisional Authority
CRSG	Country Reconstruction & Stabilization Group
DART	disaster assistance response team
DCIP	Defense Critical Infrastructure Program
DHS	Demographic Health Surveys
DFSP	Defense Fuel Support Point
DM	deutsche marks
DOD	Department of Defense
EGAT	economic growth & trade
EMI	electromagnetic interference
EMP	electromagnetic pulse
EOD	explosive ordnance disposal
EP	electrical power
EPP	Emergency Power Program
ES&CI	essential services and critical infrastructure
GER	gross enrolment ratio
GIS	geographic information system
HA	humanitarian assistance
HAZMAT	Hazardous material
H-CMIC	Handbook Civil-Military Cooperation
HDI	human development indicators
HN	HN
HVAC	heating, ventilation, and air conditioning
ICAF	Interagency Conflict Assessment Framework
IDP	internally displaced person population
IG	inspector general
IMS	interagency management system
IPC	Integration Planning Cell

IT	information technology
IQC	Indefinite Quantities Contracting
kV	kilo Volt
kVA	kilo Volt-Amps
LDC	local distribution company
LOE	line of effort
MCF/D	thousands of cubic feet per day
ME	micro-enterprises
MEPS	mobile electrical power supplies
MME	main mission element
MPICE	measuring progress in conflict environments
NATO	North Atlantic Treaty Organization
KCI&KA	national critical infrastructure and key assets
NGO	nongovernmental organization
OECD	Organization for Economic Cooperation and Development
OFDA	Office of US Foreign Disaster Assistance
OMB	Office of Management and Budget
OYB	operating year budget
PBLSC	performance based lump-sum contract
POC	point of contact
PRT	provincial reconstruction team
PSN	public switch switched network
PSP	private sector participation
RFI	radio frequency interference
SADI	system average interrupt duration index
SAIFI	system average interrupt frequency index
SCADA	supervisory control and data acquisition
S/CRS	State Department of the Coordinator for Reconstruction and Stabilization
SIGIR	Special Inspector General for Iraq Reconstruction
SME	subject-matter expert
SPF	single point of failure
TOA	transfer of authorities; transition of authority
TPEAS	total primary energy supply
TRADOC	United States Army Training and Doctrine Command
UN	United Nations
UNDP	United Nations development programme

UNHCR	United Nations Office of the High Commissioner for Refugees
UPS	uninterrupted power supplies
USACE	United States Army Corps of Engineers
USAID	United States Agency for International Development
USCAPOC	United States Army Civil Affairs and Psychological Operations Command
USG	United States Government

Intentionally Blank

Handbook for Military Support to ES&CI

PART II—DEFINITIONS

corporate governance. The overarching term that defines the set of relationships between a company's management, its board, its shareholders and other stakeholders. It provides the structure through which the objectives of the company are set, and the means of attaining those objectives and monitoring performance are determined.

cost recovery. Full cost recovery means recovering or funding the full costs of a project or service. In addition to the costs directly associated with the project, such as staff and equipment, projects will also draw on the rest of the organization. For example, adequate finance, human resources, management, and IT systems, are also integral components of any project or service. The full cost of any project therefore includes an element of each type of overhead cost, which should be allocated on a comprehensive, robust, and defensible basis. (Source: The Association of Chief Executives of Voluntary Organizations [UK])

customer-facing functions. Those actions in which business interacts directly with its customer base. Examples include billing and collections, customer service, installation and repair, etc.

golden hour. Derived from the medical context of the immediate post-triage period, the golden hour is that period of time (of whatever duration) immediately following an intervention or conclusion of a crisis, when authority structures, customary relationships, and familiar procedures have come unmoored from civil society. Decisions made during this period will have far-reaching impact by becoming the new standard around which a fractured society will coalesce as they reorganize themselves for the future. Popular tolerance of outside entities is usually higher during this period. In the context of a post-conflict environment, it can last up to a year following the initial intervention.

national critical infrastructure and key assets. The infrastructure and assets vital to a nation's security, governance, public health and safety, economy, and public confidence. They include telecommunications, electrical power systems, gas and oil distribution and storage, water supply systems, banking and finance, transportation, emergency services, industrial assets, [health & welfare] information systems, and continuity of government operations. Also called **NCI&KA**. (Source: JP 3-26)

natural monopoly. The most commonly cited examples of natural monopolies are utilities such as railroads, pipelines, electric power transmission systems and water supply systems. Such industries are characterized by very large costs for their infrastructure (i.e., which are *fixed costs*), and it is thus often *inefficient* (i.e., detrimental to the economy as a whole) to have more than a single firm in a region because of the high cost of duplicating the facilities (e.g., parallel pipelines or parallel sets of electric wires to every home and business).

operating margins. Calculated by deducting operating expenses (e.g. cost of goods and services, sales and marketing, general and administration, and depreciation and amortization of assets) from total revenues. It is an important measurement of management's efficiency, and also the profitability and performance of a company or enterprise. A company having a higher operating margin on average than its industry competitor's, tends to have better gross margins and lower fixed costs, thereby giving management more flexibility in influencing prices. Also known as Operating profit margin or Net profit margin. Operating margin = Operating income/Total revenue (Source: InvestorDictionary.com).

platform. Term widely used within the development community; a basis, a foundation, a cognitive schema, the underlying principle; the organizational scheme from which programs are managed. In this context, it is not a physical unit per normal military use.

recovery investment plan. The outline of investment decisions to improve an under-performing or non-functioning utility sector.

shareholders. A person or entity who owns shares in a corporation.

single point of failure. That portion of a system, either mechanical or organizational, the failure of which will cause the entire system to fail. To compensate for this threat, designers build in system redundancies or create a controlled progression of failure modes. There can be more than one SPF in a given system. Also called **SPF**.

stakeholders. Project stakeholders are those entities within or without an organization which. a) Sponsor a project or, b) Have an interest or a gain upon a successful completion of a project. (Source. InvestorDictionary.com)

state-owned enterprises. A corporation or business owned by the government, and thus subject to management considerations colored by political priorities as opposed to focusing on efficient product delivery and profit. Also called **SOE**.

transparency. Openness and clarity in accounting and financing, or other decisions; allows for accurate and timely monitoring and direction of business enterprises by management, regulators, shareholders and stakeholders.